Ellenville
High
School

COPING

WITH

A Physically

Challenged

Brother or

Sister

COPING

WITH

A Physically

Challenged

Brother or

362.4
RAT

Sister

Linda Lee Ratto, M. Ed.

THE ROSEN PUBLISHING GROUP, INC./ NEW YORK

Published in 1992 by The Rosen Publishing Group, Inc.
29 East 21st Street, New York, NY 10010

Copyright 1992 by Linda Lee Ratto, M. Ed.

First Edition

Library of Congress Cataloging-in-Publication Data

Ratto, Linda Lee.
  Coping with a physically challenged brother or sister / Linda
Lee Ratto. -- 1st ed. p. cm.
  Includes bibliographical references and index.
  Summary: Young people talk about how they feel as siblings of
the physically handicapped.
  ISBN 0-8239-1492-5
  1. Physically handicapped children--Family relationships--
Juvenile literature. 2. Brothers and sisters--Juvenile literature.
  [1. Physically handicapped. 2. Brothers and sisters.] I. Title.
HV903.R38 1992
362.4'043--dc20
                                                    92-3533
                                                      CIP
                                                       AC

Manufactured in the United States of America

For David, Courtney, Eric,
Ryan, and Me

ABOUT THE AUTHOR ◇

Linda Lee Ratto is a mother of three and a teacher of preschool, elementary, and secondary students. She has written a dozen picture books, young people's chapter storybooks, and young adult books on the physically challenged.

Mrs. Ratto has a Bachelor of Science Degree in English and Education and a Master of Science in Reading Education. She took up journal-writing as therapy when her first child, Courtney, was born. Courtney, now thirteen, was born without a left hand. As she grew, her mother wrote a new book every year or so, explaining the many phases and experiences Courtney was going through. Beginning with a photo-essay on how a hook-prosthesis looks and works, Courtney has become her mother's editor. She reads the work and tells Mom if the feelings and explanations are accurate and easily understood. In this way not only does Courtney express her feelings, but Mrs. Ratto comes to understand more about her daughter.

Following two mastectomies, chemotherapy, and breast reconstruction, Mrs. Ratto became personally aware of how an amputee feels. She counsels women all over the world on how to cope through the cancer experience, as well as writing articles for newspapers and magazines.

After her youngest son, Ryan, was blinded in one eye in an accident, the Rattos learned more closely how tragedy can affect every single member of a family. Ryan and his mother have written a young reader about the parts of the eye and the accident.

Mrs. Ratto is a national public speaker. She conducts educational seminars and workshops for children and adults, focusing on physicians, nurses, and other medical personnel. She has been guest speaker on many television and radio programs, advocating patient education and patient management of one's own health.

Courtney and her mother teach science units on "Prostheses as Tools," bringing in all her outgrown hook-prostheses for young people to try on. Having taught in New York, Delaware, Pennsylvania, and Georgia, they find young people to be fascinated with the unit. They plan another course on the electronic, five-fingered hand Courtney will receive next year. The Rattos believe that through education society will become more understanding and accepting of the differences in people.

Our Family History (Preface)

Feeling special is what every child needs to grow up into a confident adult. Adults need to feel special as well, or their confidence can die. When my first child, Courtney, was born without a left hand, my husband and I determined to make her feel special and confident right from the start. One of the reasons we decided to have two more children was to make sure Courtney was part of a situation that is normal in life: You aren't the only one! We wanted her to learn that there was more to life than her one-handedness. Let's face it, we were all born into a world with billions of other people! Having brothers and sisters helps us learn to share, learn to live side by side on this earth.

And so Courtney's brothers came along and simply accepted Courtney and her prosthesis because she had always been that way. Sure they fought, as all children do. But they had more to fuss about than Courtney's prosthesis. That one part of her, the one-handedness, was far from their minds on most playdays. They live a life of sharing, the way big families usually do.

All of Courtney's frequent visits to the doctors and prosthetists were made to be pleasant experiences for her. Usually lunch or a quick trip to a favorite park was part of the day off from school. Eric and Ryan were given other special "days-out" that we call "dates" so that they too could feel special having a fun experience alone with Mom.

Then Ryan had an accident. He was blinded in his left eye. Month after month, surgery after surgery, our family was thrown into sadness and confusion. Time away at the hospital caused the children left at home almost to wish it could happen to them so they could have their parents' undivided attention! Imagine that, *wishing* you could be in the hospital, wishing you could be the one hurt.

This book is about the brothers and sisters (siblings) of physically challenged people. Although they don't have an injury or physical pain, although they don't have a problem with hearing or walking or learning, they do experience *inner* pain. This book is meant to try to understand the hurt that is involved when a family has to face a challenge to the health and well-being of one of its members. Brothers and sisters of the physically challenged feel their sibling's pain, they share their sibling's struggles, and many times they are as distressed and saddened about the daily challenges to be faced as is their brother or sister. Every member of a family *lives* the challenges the other family members are experiencing. Every one in the family must change too. Every family member needs to take care and take the time to be treated well—and with specialness. Often the pain and confusion of the uninjured, the non-physically challenged brother or sister, is not understood or simply overlooked. But isn't emotional pain as important to relieve as physical pain? I think so.

Thus, this book is written especially for those who share a life with a physically challenged person. It is my hope that you understand that you are not alone in your feelings, that you *do count*, that you need to understand and to be understood. And last, but most important of all, know that you are just as special in your own ways as your brother or sister. Please read this book and cry. Cry for all the sadness you've felt that has gone unnoticed. Cry for your brother or sister and what they have to go through. Cry for yourself and how you wish your life were different . . . Then dry your tears and look at what you do have. Day by day, look at your life and your brother's or sister's life. *We are alive.* We *are* able. We do have successes *daily*! After the tears, decide to see that a glass of water is *half full*, rather than *half empty*. Decide to be happier.

Contents

CHAPTER 1

The Change

Ladasha

My dad just left us. He and Mom have been fighting ever since my baby brother went deaf in the hospital. He was so sick with the flu that he got dehydrated, and they put him in the hospital on an IV to fill him back up with fluids and fight his fever. He's only five. But the flu virus did something crazy, and now he can't hear anybody or anything. Dad told Mom and me last night that he couldn't stand it any more and was moving out. I can't believe it. I didn't think I could cry any more tears after I heard about my baby brother, but now I can't sleep because I can't stop crying. How can my father leave us at a time like this? How will we live and care for my brother? He's going to have to go to a special and very expensive private school for the deaf. Mom may have to change jobs just to be able to drive him to and from that school. Now Dad will have to spend half of our money getting his own place. Why can't he just love us and be with us during this awful tragedy in our lives?

Carlos

After my sister was in that car accident, I had to go to work. I'm only thirteen, but we can't afford the doctor's bills if I don't. My mother goes straight from work to the hospital every evening. While she's at the hospital, I either have to take care of my two brothers or I go off to the gas station to work. I look older than thirteen; I lied on the application, and they hired me without checking me out. I take the cash from the gas customers. It's boring, but at least I can help. My mother is so down, I can't ever tell her how tired I get. She barely makes it to the table for a bite to eat after hospital visits. Most of the time she comes home, reports on my sister while she drinks a cup of tea, hugs me, and goes to bed. My sister is paralyzed from the waist down. She's only nine. We need to pay the hospital bill tomorrow when she comes home. I hope we have enough money for a wheelchair. My mother applied for welfare last week. Even with my check, we won't be able to keep up with her care at home if we don't have medical help. It'll never be the same around here, but I don't think about that. I don't think about much. I just go to school, do my homework, visit my sister on weekends with my brothers, and go to work four nights a week. At least two of the work nights are on the weekends. Sometimes I am so tired I fall asleep in class. Maybe I should just quit school and work full time. I could help out so much more with that extra full-time cash.

Major Changes

When a family experiences a major catastrophe, it can be devastating in more ways than you ever thought when the tragedy first happened. It is quite common for every single family member to suffer in significant ways.

A Parent Can Leave

Often when a crisis strikes a family, one of the parents simply cannot handle the situation and leaves. To the rest of the world, and especially to his or her children, this seems like the very last thing a parent could do. But it happens. It happens because the pain of seeing a loved one in agonizing change is too much for that parent to live with. So he or she chooses to leave.

It may be the right decision for him or her. But what about the rest of the family?

Try to Understand

There are some things we may never fully understand about the people around us, but we must try to look at things from other people's points of view. Ladasha is just looking through Ladasha's eyes right now. She sees how hard it is and will be. She must look at her dad with an understanding that he too is hurting inside. He is hurting so badly emotionally that he had to leave. He does not know how to cope with his family's problems.

This is an important example of a time when a family needs a counselor. In trying to communicate and then learn to cope with the trauma of a child's losing his hearing, all of the family members must work hard. These are the times when all our inner strength must come through for us, along with our patience. A family needs to understand that *every* member will have to lean on the others at some point during the long crisis period. If Dad must leave for a while, so be it. But do not give up. Try to get help from a church, a school, or a medical team to help you understand. Usually the person leaving a situation loves his family so much that he cannot bear the pain. Rather than hating her dad for leaving, Ladasha must look at *her* pain and understand that everyone in her family is feeling pain right along with her baby brother. Adults have hearts that break too. During a crisis, there is no extra energy left in anyone's body for hate. You're all too tired to use your energy for anything but good things. *Trying* to understand is the first step in the painful process of coping with family change. Trying is the first step toward understanding.

Trauma Causes Personal Hardship

Carlos is a fine, upstanding young man who is doing all he can to help his sister, mother, and two brothers. But if he does not begin to be honest about how he is feeling, the next thing he may see is his *own* sickness. It is wonderful for a family to pull together during a major time of need. Working extra hours, doing more than has been the norm are constructive ways to use the energy that makes us lose sleep during a family trauma. It is good to work things out through keeping busy. But that kind of superhuman effort has to slow down gradually, day by day. As the family readjusts and learns to realize that Carlos's sister will not be able to walk for a while, Carlos will have to change his crisis routine to a daily routine that allows him to continue school yet still earn extra money. Giving to your family in every way is wonderful, but you must not give away the important things that are yours: health, education, a friend to talk to, time to relax a little and step back and breathe. Taking care of your own major personal needs is a present you give to everyone around you. If you are well, you can help your family out in a better and stronger way. When family members are overtired and depriving themselves, they tend to fight. During a time of trauma, fighting just creates more problems.

Communicating

Carlos and Ladasha must begin to get their feelings out. Finding a trusted friend to discuss your troubles with is a great way to help cope. Getting your feelings out in conversation or writing in a journal or diary will help organize your thoughts. When you are less confused, you will feel better and your situation will improve. Carlos must begin to talk to his mother. If he went to the hospital coffee shop and asked his mother to come for some time together, that would be a beginning to more communication. Yes, his mother is depressed, but so is Carlos. Crisis is a time to share feelings, not to walk into your own little world and hate the outside.

Ladasha must also seek to tell someone her feelings, her fears about her father's leaving. A school counselor is an excellent person to turn to if your own family or friends don't seem to be enough. That is why school guidance people are hired, paid by your family's school taxes: to listen when you need help. Teachers are a good source of contact if you don't feel comfortable just dropping by the counselor's office. Trusted church members and neighbors may also be able to connect you with people who counsel others in need. When things at home become confusing and more than you can take, communicating clears your mind. Write in your diary, talk to someone you like who you know can help.

CHAPTER 2

It's Always Been This Way

Eric

Since I'm younger than my sister, I've just always lived with the fact that she was born with only one hand. Sometimes she seems to get away with things, like taking time off from school to get fitted for a new prosthesis. She gets to skip school and have lunch out, and she always seems so happy when I come home from the school-bus stop. I hate that part. But sometimes Mom takes me places by myself too. I get to eat where I want to and do one activity of my choice. Those are my favorite days in the whole world, taking days off with Mom or Dad all by myself! When I was little I used to wish I had a nice metal hook-tool like my sister's prosthesis. Then I could act like Superman and really bop my enemies! But I'm eleven now, and I know I'd rather have two hands. Sometimes I put my hand in my pocket and pretend I don't have fingers or a hand on that side like my sister. Then I remind myself how lucky I am to have all my body parts. But I do hate it when we have to save money and not go to the movies as much because we have to save for my sister's next prosthesis. Every one of her artificial hands costs thousands of dollars! My parents' medical plan pays for only 80 percent of the prosthetist's bill. We have to pay the rest. As she gets older, the bigger prostheses cost more, and she gets a new one about every year. So part of each year I get kind of mad that things aren't "normal" for her so we could spend the money on fun stuff.

One really great thing though, next year she's getting a myoelectronic, five-fingered hand! She'll have an actual robotic hand! We've been saving up for it, and she is so excited because she'll be able to wear rings on that hand. She'll even be able to paint the fingernails on the flesh-colored glove that goes over the electronic parts. Mom is going to take us along when they start fitting her. I can't wait to go back into Mr. Danny's workroom and watch him start making it. It is so cool! He begins by measuring her hand and the length of her full-sized arm; then he puts a full cast over her residual limb (non-handed arm). He will fill the cast with wax to make a mold. The mold will be used to form plastic into a perfectly shaped socket that will fit on the end of her arm and hold the electronic-hand for her use.

I guess most of the time I don't think about my sister being physically challenged, I just fight with her and get along with her and think she's an okay sister. She's normal in lots of other ways, you know. But when we go swimming in the neighborhood pool and she doesn't have her prosthesis on, sometimes I feel sad for her. She'll never have a real left hand. But she's pretty nice and I'm glad she's my sister. And she's the fastest swimmer in our whole family!

Kasib

My brother has asthma. He goes to the hospital at least once a year. He has to sleep in a special bedroom with a tent over the bed, because when he gets an infection it's hard for him to breathe. Mom and Dad have to make sure he breathes as much oxygen as he can, so we have oxygen tanks delivered to the house and he uses them when he has a bad breathing spell. You know, if you don't get enough oxygen to the brain, you can have brain damage. My brother's in the hospital now; he developed pneumonia. But he's feeling much better. I wish I could go to the hospital and get a few new games and toys and baked treats from everybody we know! A lot of times on school nights I have to stay home with a baby-sitter even though I'm already ten. Mom and Dad both go to the hospital and there I am, watching boring TV while they have a party in my brother's room with my aunts and uncles, eating cakes and cookies and laughing. I wish I'd get sick and be in the hospital for a whole month! My brother's always been this way with his breathing problems, and I hate it.

Accepting Differences

Eric has a different attitude from Ladasha and Carlos. He has always lived with his sister's difference. He accepts her. The changes his parents had to experience were long ago, before he was born. His parents have tried to make him feel as special as his sister, and it shows. He cares for his sister, and most of the time he isn't jealous of the time she has with their parents when she has appointments with medical support people. Eric has grown from being a little boy who wished he had a tool like his sister's prosthesis, to understanding with a bit of sadness that she will never have a left hand. It seems as if he's actually getting excited and happy *with* her as he and his family prepare for the purchase of a myoelectronic hand. Sure, he always wishes they'd have more money to spend on things *he* wants, but don't we all feel that way at times?

Wishing for the Worst

It was a sign of lacking something when Eric wished he could have a prosthesis like his sister's. Imagine wishing not to have one of your hands so you could have a neat tool. Or imagine wanting to be sick in the hospital so your parents would hold a party for you, as Kasib wishes. Wishing you could be like a physically challenged relative is a sign that something is not right in your life. Look at what that wish would honestly mean: Eric's hand would have to be amputated for his parents to get him a prosthetic hand. Is that really what Eric wants? No, Eric wants the neat new toy his sister gets every year. He wants to take days off from school as often as possible. Days off are great, aren't they? And wishing for sickness is not the best way to get what Kasib needs, either. He needs attention. His parents and family members have been doing nothing but fuss over his brother. He's jealous! So jealous that he wants to be ill too. Kasib must talk to his family and let his feelings be known. He must ask for time alone with his parents. When he has a little time with them, he won't wish to be sick any more. He'll feel loved again.

Wishes and Permanence

The special thing about wishing for something is that it is not a real happening. A wish that you were your brother or sister so you could get what they seem to have won't come true. If it did come true, you'd *be* like your brother or sister, and in many ways that is *not* what you really want. Physical challenges often are permanent. As a brother or sister of a physically challenged person, it is important to remember that he may improve but never get to the way your body is. Eric's sister can never touch things on the left side of her body, never have a left hand. That is her body, and wishing for it is not what Eric wants to do. If you want attention, if you want to take a day off, write your parents a note and ask them for time together. Use your thoughts to try to tell your family how much you like being with them and that not being with them in special ways makes you unhappy. Communication, again, is a tool for your own happier future. Change your wishes to things that you can make come true, then work toward your positive dreams.

How About A Health Party?

Maybe Kasib could suggest that his family have a big party when his brother comes home. Kasib could be in charge of the party, preparing food, going to the market for favorite fruits and goodies. He could make a list and invite the guests with invitations and everything. Kasib would be a major reason for the party; he would be the organizer, the "doer." The event would not only make Kasib's brother feel terrific, but it would make Kasib a part of his brother's treatment and of his brother's life.

His parents would be proud, and everyone would have a great time being together.

Celebrating for a physically challenged sibling is a must. Certainly coming home from a hospital stay is an excellent reason to party. But celebrating often for any success is a great way for a family to acknowledge the special joys in their lives. The parties and celebrations should be for any of the family members and their accomplishments! If you look toward the positive side of every day, you'll find all sorts of reasons to bake a cake, go to a favorite sporting event, or invite some relatives over. Accenting the positives will make every family member feel better!

CHAPTER 3

Shock, Denial, and Anger

nger is a very strong, very human emotion, felt by all of us at one time or another. Anger is one of the first stages of grief discussed in Elisabeth Kübler-Ross' book *On Death and Dying*. It is normal to feel angry that your brother or sister is physically challenged. All of the stages of grief and the feelings that come when tragedy strikes a home are normal for any one of us to feel. In other words, it is all right to feel what you feel.

It would be helpful to define grief as in the Webster dictionaries:

> Grief: emotional suffering caused by an unfortunate outcome; distress over a disaster or a death.

Denying the Truth

Let's look at the first stage of grief. Dr. Kübler-Ross was the first physician to name the stages of human behavior in grief. The first is denying that anything is different and then staying away from the situation, avoiding thinking about the change or avoiding the very person who is going through the trauma. Having a physically challenged member of the family does not mean that the person has died, but the brother or sister who used to be, or could have been, *has* died.

The idea that a person could run a marathon after being paralyzed from the waist down is not realistic. The person who used to run well has died. In his or her place is a changed person, one who can no longer run. When a family member does not want to admit that her relative has changed, that person is not growing. She is denying that the relative has changed. Seeing only the way a physically challenged person *used* to be is denial. Often a sibling does not even want to see the patient, not want to discuss the accident or disease or birth that caused the disabling of that family member.

Denial can happen to any member of the family. Look at Ladasha's father. He is stuck in the first stage of grief; he is so pained by the realization that his child is deaf that he feels he must isolate himself from that child. He may have finally accepted the truth of his child's disability but is unable to go further and grow with his family. So he has left. He is isolating himself from his son and the rest of his family.

Understanding Can Lead to Anger

Ladasha and Kasib are at the second stage of grief, anger. They both understand that their brothers are hurt and have changed. Ladasha is angry at her father for leaving. Kasib is angry at his parents for not including him when they visit his brother. It doesn't seem as though either

Ladasha or Kasib is angry at the brother, yet their anger really stems from the challenging situation their brothers are going through. How could they get rid of their anger?

Jeremiah

I've been assigned in-school suspension ten times since school started this year and it isn't even Christmas vacation yet. I get in trouble all the time. People say stuff about my sister and her leg braces, and I just want to *kill* them. I feel the anger blow up inside my head and chest. I fight back. I've hit some guys right in their filthy mouths. I mean I want to protect my sister. She tries her best. At least she can walk now. She was born with a hole in her spine, with part of the spine growing out of the hole (it's called spina bifida). She's had three operations to remove the tumor-like bump that was on her back when she was born. But the nerves in her spine were damaged, and the doctors said she wouldn't be able to walk. My parents got braces to help make her legs stronger, and they took her to physical therapy from the time she was a year old. And she learned to walk! She still goes to rehabilitation therapy every week. She works really hard, doing her exercises every day. She doesn't like the way her braces look, so she wears pants or longer skirts to hide them. But she still gets noticed because she walks slightly bent over and can't climb stairs very well. Some of the kids are so cruel. They call her names right in front of me. What am I supposed to do but smash their heads in?

Listen to Your Body

Hendrie Weisinger, Ph.D., author of *Dr. Weisinger's Anger Work-Out Book*, tells many ways you can help yourself work through your anger. He tells of the importance of realizing how your body feels when you start getting angry. To better understand that "moment of anger," reread Jeremiah's story. He describes the "blowing-up" inside his head and chest. You know that feeling. We all do. You know that if you keep thinking angry thoughts your face gets hot and sweaty. Inside your swelling chest, as you continue to go over and over the angry thoughts and the "good" reasons for the angry thoughts, your heart races faster. If you don't do something you feel as if you could *kill*! And you certainly can't do that. Yet if you do nothing at all, if you keep these strong, gripping body reactions swallowed inside, you will eventually get very, very sick. All those negative thoughts have to get out. It's like a small infection in a cut: If you don't get it cleaned out, your whole body can eventually become infected. The same is true with negative energy from angry feelings. Stomachaches, ulcers, headaches, heart problems, blood-pressure problems can all come from swallowing, rather than letting out, your anger.

Try Control

If you have ever felt anger, you know what it feels like. Try paying attention to yourself when something or someone sets your anger going. Try *thinking* about your feelings. Ask yourself if getting mad is really worth all the energy you're going to use. Is the reason worth it? Try breathing slowly and very deeply, still thinking. Perhaps you'll decide that some of the things that used to make you angry aren't worth it. You know that your physically challenged sibling is not to blame. He or she is just the way he or she is. That is life. What are you going to *choose* to do about it: make life uncomfortable for your own body and everybody else's? Think. Many times if you think while these angry feelings are beginning, you can stop them. It's easy, but it takes practice. Try thinking today. Try learning today, in place of just reacting.

Some Ways to Get Rid of Anger

You're human. You're not perfect. Let's say you are trying very hard not to become angry because for the hundredth time you can't do something you want to do because you have to help your physically challenged sibling. What now? How can you still get into control? How can you melt your anger away when it has already swelled inside you?

The Better-Way Chart

On the opposite page is a chart of positive and negative ways to deal with anger. Positive ways help a person grow through his anger, and he gets rid of it because he has learned. Negative ways of handling anger cause other problems. Negative ways can make anger grow stronger, because the person has more and more things to be angry about. That is a negative way to grow.

Coping Well

A definition of coping is needed to keep things clear:

Cope: to contend with difficulties and act to over-
come them; to strive to learn through tragedy
with success.

Learning the good life skills to cope with tragedy is part of a mature person's success. Children cry, scream, hit, and

THE BETTER WAY CHART

NEGATIVE BEHAVIOR	>> CONSEQUENCE	POSITIVE >> ALTERNATIVE	>> BETTER RESULT/GOAL
Hate a family member	Causes more sadness	Talk out your angry feelings	Your family members understand and you deal with your anger
Fight out your anger, hit people who make fun	Hurts others Gets you in trouble for breaking the rules	Ignore mean comments Explain why your relative is the way he/she is	You won't get into a fight and hurt them Others will learn to understand differences rather than make fun and hurt feelings
Scream and yell at everyone because your family is going through a hard year	You'll lose friends People won't want to be around you You'll get very lonely and more unhappy	Take a jog when you want to lash out at others; think: "Get out anger" Count to ten before you speak, then *explain* how you're feeling	You'll feel better and the anger will be much less; no one gets hurt Being patient helps you think; if you explain your feelings, you'll understand them better
You are so confused you can't think, you can't do your work, you snap at everyone	You hurt others You stay confused	Take a time-out, go to a quiet room, write your confused thoughts down Take a walk and think Count to a number until calmer	You won't hurt others Everyone needs time alone Writing thoughts helps make them clear Exercise gets sad feelings out Slowing down to think works

kick. They just react. More mature people learn something from most experiences. Mature people do not hurt others' bodies or feelings, even during a crisis. If they do hurt someone, they realize it and apologize. Mature and growing human beings explain their feelings to others so as to develop understanding. This behavior saves us from war.

Let's Live Well

Learning to live well means trying to see the positive in things, even when you are feeling at your worst. It is normal to have feelings. Anger is a strong human emotion. In the days of early man, anger was shown by striking out. Many of us have that first reaction. But we live *with others*. In a civilized world we must find other ways to handle our normal feelings of anger besides hitting people and causing daily wars with our neighbors. The chart shows only a few practical ways to get rid of your anger and still get along with others. The rest of this book offers many other choices of ways to deal with your emotions.

Getting Rid of Anger by Forgiving

We must all recognize angry feelings and work on getting rid of them. If we do not find a way to get rid of our anger, we may get sick or become handicapped mentally. If you hold a grudge against someone and do not forgive him or her, the grudge will prevent you from doing things. That is being handicapped mentally. You are not free because your anger is blocking your freedom to *like others*. That can lead to illness and isolation. Let's face it, no one wants to be with an angry person for very long.

What sensible student would want to be around Jeremiah with his reputation for fighting? If he does not get rid of his anger, he will soon be friendless or hurt himself or others severely. He must forgive. Jeremiah must forgive the people who say things he doesn't like about his sister. Those people don't know. They may even be afraid, because they don't understand how it is to wear braces all day, every day. Maybe they wonder what if it happened to them? Those are scary thoughts. Jeremiah would do well to begin explaining what a strong person his sister is, how much she has to practice during therapy just to continue walking. People are ignorant of situations they have never seen or experienced. They have a different point of view. We all have different points of view. That is not wrong. Although saying hateful things is wrong, people simply do not understand when they say those things.

Getting Help

What if Jeremiah cannot bring himself even to talk to those students who don't understand how their words hurt? What if Ladasha decides never to talk to her father again? What then? Anger that is held inside can become so big, so full, that all a person feels is anger. That is the time to get help. A professional counselor can help you train yourself in the life skills needed to release and control your anger. Learning about anger, understanding anger and why you are angry, can take time, but a system of ways to deal with angry feelings can help you live more happily for the rest of your life. Find time to ask your parent, teacher, counselor, or churchperson for help. The trusted person in your life will know what to say to comfort you or know where you can get the help you need.

The Anger Work-out

You can prevent the holding-in of negative feelings. It has been shown by many medical studies that prevention of disease and sickness from the stress of anger is possible. One of the easiest ways to set your angry feelings free is exercise. Dr. Weisinger calls people who exercise to keep anger under control, "Anger Athletes." What a name! "The Anger Athlete." How true it can be for you! A run around the block always makes a person feel better; it calms the grumblings inside. A good, hard bike ride can get your heart going, your blood flowing, and calm results! Being an "Anger Athlete" does not mean going out on the football field and crashing into everyone. It means finding an exercise that gets your heart going, that makes you sweat it all out. After the exercise, pay attention to how you feel. As you sit down with a glass of water, breathe in deeply and slowly. Feel how you feel. This is peace. It feels good. It is healthy. It hurts absolutely no one.

CHAPTER ◇ 4

Hate

Part of the angry stage of grief can be strong feelings of hate.

Anthony

I hate that we have to run our entire lives around my brother and his "condition." I'm fed up with it. It's been two years, and our family has not had a vacation. Since my brother went swimming with his friends from his junior class, dove into shallow water, and broke his neck, it's been a nightmare around here. We have to feed him, bathe him, DO, DO, DO. We hoped he would regain more use of his arms. And true, he can hold a spoon and the controls to the computer and television. He received his high school diploma this past August, just two months later than he would have if he hadn't been in the accident. And I'm proud of him for starting to take college-level courses at home. But I'm a junior now, and my life isn't my own. And I don't even do as much as my parents do for him. I just *hate it all*. I hate the guy he's turned into. One minute I'm celebrating his graduation, but the next day it's back to the grind of everyday living. Some days all I want to do is scream: "I HATE YOU, BROTHER, GET OUT OF MY LIFE!"

Hate

Anthony is so angry at the way things have gone for his brother and his family that he can barely think of anything else. Even after the accomplishment of his brother's graduation, Anthony is filled with angry words. There are two things Anthony must do to grow. He must get past this stage of anger and hate, and he must learn to get on with *his* life. Perhaps he needs to meet Kelsey or other people with physically challenged siblings.

Kelsey

I hate sticks. I hate when kids play with sticks. Sometimes you'll see me walking through the park almost yelling at kids if they even try to pick up a stick. My little brother Trevor was playing with a stick and swinging it around with another boy who also had a stick. Trevor's eye got stabbed with the stick. He's blind in that eye now. He's had four operations. My parents used almost all their savings to make sure Trevor had the best treatment in hopes of saving his sight in that eye. After two years his left eye is healthy, alive, but doesn't see anything except light and dark. I don't hate Trevor. All that we have gone through has been out of love and wanting the best for him. But I *hate* that we all had to go through this. I *hate* that the little boy who was playing with Trev won't even talk about the accident, or even what happened that day at all. I wonder how that will affect him during his life? I don't blame anyone. I hate that Trev has had so much pain, so young. I just hate that my parents have had to live through all this pain. We're a closer family because of the accident. That's good. I hug my brother more. We all hug each other more than we used to. I learned enough about eyes to write a book . . . but I just wish we never had to have this happen to us—or anybody. Life is pretty hard, isn't it?

Hate the Incident, Not the Person

Kelsey hates. But she hates certain objects, not the people who use them. We have all had the feeling of hate swell up inside us, similar to the feeling of anger. Our bodies feel the same, because anger and hate are from the same thoughts. They are parts of the same urge. You want out! Anthony wants out! He wants *no* accident, *no* daily pain, and *no* extra responsibility for anyone in his family. *No* extra responsibility for himself, either. He reacts. Although he doesn't say he has ever yelled and screamed at his brother, he is getting close . . .

The difference between Anthony's hate and Kelsey's is where it is directed. Feeling anger and hate is very normal and truly must be realized in order to let them pass. Avoiding the idea that we hate what an incident has done to us and our loved ones will only stunt our growth. The healthier way of life is to understand that you feel hate, anger, and frustration at things you cannot change, and then go on from there to live a new way of life. Blaming and hating a person only causes what that physically challenged person *does not need*—a loss of love and caring. Turning your hatred on the ones you love accomplishes two things: You get your anger and hate expressed and *out*, and your loved ones do not feel as loved any more. Are those your goals? You may say yes, you want to get your feelings out. That is a great goal. But the side effect of this hate *toward* your loved one is hurt and additional injury. This must *not* be your goal. You cannot train yourself to hurt others when you're hurting. It only causes more pain.

Focus Your Hate

Kelsey hates sticks. Yes, *sticks*. That is just fine! Sticks remind Kelsey of her brother's trauma, and so she can go ahead and hate them for the rest of her life. Her hate is focused on a *thing*, and she can live without that thing. Most of us don't even bother with sticks unless we're roasting marshmallows. But Kelsey has done herself and her brother a favor. She still loves her brother. Loving your physically challenged sibling is the important and necessary goal, especially during the difficult recovery period. Anthony and his family, unfortunately, will have a lifelong caregiving "recovery" period. That is difficult, when your own life is put on hold to help your family. Hating the *situation* is normal. Loving a person, being proud of his or her accomplishments, must be a family's crystal-clear goal. Yelling at the victim is unacceptable behavior. What should be done to free Anthony of his hate and angry feelings? Anthony should focus his anger on the accident, the shallow water, but not on his brother. Let's read about Lee.

Lee

Lee wants a motorcycle. He's seventeen and has a job that is just four miles from home. He really loves motorcycles and tells his mother how economical they are, because they get up to 50 miles per gallon of gas. He could ride to work for weeks on a tank of gas. But Lee's Uncle Billy had a terrible motorcycle accident. He was in and out of the hospital for months with both ankles and both wrists crushed. Lee's mother hates motorcycles. She used to ride them and loved the wind rushing through her hair too, but no more. Lee's mother hates motorcycles because of the pain one of them caused her brother and their entire family. Lee will not to be allowed to own one until he leaves his parents' home. Lee's mother hates motorcycles; she doesn't hate her own brother.

Hate the Incident, Not the People Involved

If a mother gives birth to a physically challenged baby, should we hate the mother? Should we hate the innocent babe? No, we shouldn't hate people. If the mother took heroin during her pregnancy, we could hate her *behavior*, but not *her*. The point about families is that we are supposed to love each other no matter what. Hating a family member for changing your life creates more tragedy. It is also rather self-centered. You are not the physically challenged person, are you? If something happened to you, wouldn't you still want to be loved?

Below is a list of suggestions for making your life a little more of what you'd like it to be. Even if you're the only one taking care of your physically challenged sibling, you can try these ideas.

1. Write a list of at least ten things you love to do but haven't had time to do.
2. Write another list of at least ten things you would like to do after the above things were done.
3. Make a list of the chores and other responsibilities you *must* do daily (example: feed pet, make lunch,

do homework, help your physically challenged sibling, do laundry).

4. Get busy after school or after your Saturday job. Do the things on the *must* list and don't dilly-dally! Get them over with. Do them happily, because you have a family and you should help as a loving member of your family. Check off everything you do. (Checking things off is a little celebration all by itself; enjoy your own small accomplishments!)

5. Now pick one fun thing from one of your first two lists. Take time to do it after your other jobs are done. Circle it on your "favorite things to do" list! Another celebration! See how many fun things you can MAKE TIME FOR in a month, and don't forget to circle them.

Here are some examples:

FAVORITE THINGS JUST FOR ME!

Favorite Things List	*2nd Favorite Things List*
1. Ride my bike	1. Read a book on a favorite subject or by a favorite author.
2. Call a friend	
3. Watch a whole television program, uninterrupted	
4. Go over to a friend's house	2. Write a letter to a best friend or special relative.
5. Make a favorite dessert	3. Play a game with your brother or sister: cards, Monopoly, whatever.
6. Go to the movies	
7. Take a long, private bath	
8. Exercise every night for 15 minutes.	4. Join a club or group and if you can't make all the meetings, that's still fine, go to most.
9. Take a long, long walk whenever I feel hateful feelings.	
	5. Buy something for yourself with saved earnings.

Favorite Things List	*2nd Favorite Things List*
10. Go with a favorite person for a shake or ice cream.	6. Plan a family day trip to a place you all enjoy; get OK from parents.
	7. Try to get your family to take a vacation . . . etc . . . etc . . .

Take Care of You Too!

As you can see, the "favorite things" idea is not expensive. There are plenty of ideas, depending on how much time you manage to put aside for *you!* Some ideas can involve your family members but in positive ways: They're *your* ideas and they're fun for all. When you find that even on a daily basis you *can* do some of what *you* want to do, you become refreshed and in control of your own life. That is an important life skill that will make you a happier person now and through adulthood. Taking care of you makes less room for hateful feelings, because you're busy making positive experiences that bring about feel-good feelings. Focus on a little fun, not what you can't change.

What about Your Parents?

What if your parents say there is no time for fun, no time for happy trips? What if your parents are caught up in paying the bills and meeting your family's needs? Try to talk more to them. Try to communicate that you feel anger and hate at times and you need a break. So do they. Read a favorite paragraph from this book, or any other article or book that supports your idea of taking time for you. Seek an adult friend's help in convincing your parents that everyone needs breaks. Time-out from serious responsibility is a must, lest resentment, anger, and hate grow and damage already traumatized lives.

Time-out Is a Gift to Yourself

Time-out need not cost anything but a little planning and reserved time. A routine time set aside to enjoy a favorite activity is a treat you can always give yourself if you decide to. Your reward is a happier you, refreshed and ready for another day. When you feel well, your world will look better. Try it!

CHAPTER ◇ 5

Jealousy and Depression

In a family with a member who is receiving most of the attention and energies, there is often jealousy. And more often than not, the word *jealous* is not considered the appropriate term for how a family member is feeling. But jealousy is at the root of many arguments and many angry feelings.

Leon

I get straight As in school, I have a part-time job at a fast-food restaurant, and I've saved a couple of thousand dollars toward college. I'm only a sophomore in high school. My parents are both professionals, and I will probably study in their footsteps and graduate with honors as a Certified Public Accountant. I love numbers. But I do not like the numbers of hours we have to spend all week, every week, taking care of my younger brother, Marcus. He has diabetes. His condition is getting worse, and he has to have dialysis three times a week now, until he can get a kidney transplant. His kidneys don't work any more. They can't filter and clean. He doesn't heal well either. If a sore gets bad enough, they may have to amputate something some day. I pray that a kidney donor is found with the right match. I cry for him almost every night. He's only ten. Then I cry for myself. Before this year when my brother's diabetes began to get worse, we were a regular family. He took insulin shots and everything was pretty fine. My parents and brother came to watch my football games on Saturdays and attended my concerts at the auditorium. I play the saxophone in the high school band. Now it's nothing but hospitals, doctors, and Marcus, Marcus, Marcus. The doctors even asked if I'd give him one of my kidneys. I wanted to, but I'm so scared of what's happening to Marcus that I can't bring myself to have surgery. Maybe that's selfish, but I don't want to die. I don't want Marcus to die either. I just want to be able to sit down for dinner like a normal family and be together. Every night it's grab a sandwich or fast food, hospital visit if it's dialysis day, or taking care of Marcus at home, then cramming in homework and studying around everything else. Thank the Lord I'm a good student, or I'd be failing this year for sure. We're not a family, we're just robots doing our jobs.

Is Thinking of Yourself Wrong?

Leon has a very difficult family situation. He is bright, intelligent, and athletic. He's healthy, and he loves his brother. But why can't he give Marcus one of his two kidneys? Leon does not want to die. He is scared. He's afraid that he might die himself, giving a kidney to Marcus. Leon loves life, at least the way life was before his brother got so sick. But now he's jealous of the time taken away from his football and music, and he is very unhappy. He is torn between love of his family, fear of what is happening to his brother, and memories of better times for his family. Leon is acting a bit immature and self-centered during this tragedy. He is also becoming depressed, feeling there's no way out!

Feelings Are Normal

It is normal and right to have strong feelings in defense of yourself when a trauma hits your family. In *Helping Your Child Handle Stress*, Dr. Katharine Kersey tells of introducing a new baby into a family. She cites normal regression of behavior in the siblings when the baby arrives. Trauma is similar to a new birth: the birth of a big change in a family's life. Leon, although usually mature, is going back inside himself a little and wants what *he* wants. He has become self-centered partly because he doesn't have as much attention as he used to. He feels a little unloved. Dr. Kersey says that when a big change takes place in a family we should expect some less mature behavior. It is natural to be tired of it all, want things to be the way they were, and want your parents' undivided attention once in a while.

Looking back at Chapter 4, the need to take care of yourself has been pointed out. Some people, like Leon, have a natural instinct to defend their inner selves. This is positive, because Leon is an excellent survivor. The people around him must understand and accept his decision not to give his kidney to his brother. Leon is healthy. He's crying out that he needs a break. Others must be persuaded to take time out, as well.

Stages of Grief

Leon is a good example of the third and fourth stages of grief. Dr. Kübler-Ross says that after the anger there is a stage of bargaining and guilt, followed by depression. Leon is experiencing that now. On the one hand he loves Marcus and wants to help him. Yet he also feels guilty about not wanting to give Marcus one of his kidneys. These feelings are leading him to an uncomfortable feeling that there is no way out. When people feel there is no way out, they are becoming depressed. They will become more sad and depressed if a change does not take place. Leon needs help right now in seeing some light in his dark-seeming life.

Tiffany

I get up with the first ray of sunshine. I shower, wash my hair, and go over the chapters I know will be on my next quiz. I dress, eat a quick breakfast, and get Brett his cereal while I put away the clean dishes out of the dishwasher. By this time, my mother is almost ready to grab her shower, since it usually takes her a half hour to dress Brett, or at least supervise his dressing. My older brother has Down syndrome. He's twenty now. Dad left when Mom found out she was pregnant with me. It's been the three of us for almost eighteen years. I'll be graduating in June, but I'll go to a nearby college and live at home. I don't know whether I'll ever move out of the house. Mom has so much to do, and between us we have managed pretty well helping Brett. Brett has been in a day-home to graduate him into the community, but he hasn't been able to keep a job yet. I hope he'll be able to soon. For now, Mom and I split driving him to and from the community home. He loves his room here and doesn't really sleep well in other places. I've had a part-time job (full-time in the summer) since I was thirteen, packing groceries or checking-out at the local food store. I've saved enough to go to the community college for two years! Then I'll continue on to our local four-year college, probably taking out a school loan and working too. I'm going to be a nurse. Let's face it, I've been doing it all my life! Brett has a moderate form of Down's but has learned so much more than some of his friends at the home. I think it's because he's had so much love and care from Mom and me.

Tiffany is an example of someone who has no jealousy, perhaps because she's never had her mother all to herself as Leon did. Brett has always been a part of Tiffany's life. She simply accepts him, loves him, and helps him. That is beautiful. Her mother has not had a husband all these years and has needed Tiffany. They have made a terrific team, and Brett's ability to learn is the payoff for their hard work and loving care. But Tiffany does not see herself ever having a life of her own. Her "self" has not developed very much. She is caught up in her brother's and mother's needs. Her plan is not to leave home, even when she goes to college. She plans to become a nurse, but there is a sense that it is all for her family.

Striking a Balance

Leon and Tiffany exemplify the two ends of a large scale of helpfulness. See the diagram below to understand the importance of balancing your life with others' lives.

THE
HAPPY
MEDIUM
———
some time out
every day
———
some personal goals
of your own
———

Tiffany
(few personal desires)

Leon
(wants total time-out)

Leon has many ideas for himself apart from his brother and parents. As one grows into maturity, that is an important way to be. It is the way a person needs to be to make it on his own, living independently.

Tiffany has not allowed herself time even to think of herself. At almost eighteen, she is already behind in her life-curve of growth. She has a goal: to be a nurse, but she has not given any thought to life apart from her mother and brother. That is somewhat immature for her age. Normally, teens dream of life on their own. Tiffany needs time-out. Tiffany must learn to dream—and date!

You Have a Life

In Robin Simons's book *After the Tears*, she discusses all the stormy emotions involved within the family when caring for a disabled child. She discusses the importance of balance, the importance of having a life outside the family as well as within. It is normal to be resentful, as Leon is, because his family hasn't been able to go to his school activities. It is normal for Tiffany to want to help her family as much as she possibly can. But there must be limits because you have been given a life of your own to live. Tiffany should be encouraged to go out on her own, perhaps after she completes her two-year degree. Maybe Tiffany's family could all work toward the goal of independence for Brett, Tiffany, and their mother. Teamwork within the family makes life so much better and stronger. But the goal of living well independently is one we all should have.

CHAPTER ◇ 6

Communication
and a Change
in Attitude

Unlock the door to your dreams. Try to communicate with your family members in a way that you never have before. Here are some ideas for you to try. If you try them all and they don't work, try them again! Some things may not work at certain times. Think about the timing of your communication, how you say it, the tone of voice you use.

Hints for Better Communication

1. Ask for a night out alone with one of your parents. Explain that you feel jealous of all the special time and care everyone is giving to your sibling. Don't forget to say that you love being with them, that you love their attention.

2. Write a card or note saying that you'd like to talk to your loved one. Make the card yourself, and include some hearts.
3. If you get caught in a shouting match, try to stop and think. Realize that everyone must be tired, everyone needs a time-out. Now tell whomever you're fighting with that you're tired and would like to take a little walk. Setting an example can teach others a lot.
4. Choose a night that is not as busy as most and suggest setting that evening aside for things done by you and your dad or you and your mom. If both parents live with you, set aside two nights. Stick to the nights, look forward to them, plan for them.
5. Suggest that you buy a 1,000-piece jigsaw puzzle and come home and begin it. Find a place to keep it so you can work on it until it is complete. You may even want to glue it on a board and frame it. Be proud!
6. Have your parent read aloud some chapters of the book you're reading. You could read every other chapter aloud together.
7. Play cards, or a board game, or perhaps learn a new game.
8. Go to a movie, but prepare for it—discuss with your parent or sibling which one you both want to see. Make it an event, a special matinee (usually they're half price!) or evening. Fun time is needed as well as serious time.
9. Take a very long walk, perhaps to a place to have a treat with one of your parents.
10. Save your money and go shopping with one of your parents. Buy a treat for your parent after

you've purchased your items. Treat your parents
the way you'd like to be treated; spoil them with
your personal attention!

It's All in Your Attitude

Attitude. You've heard that word a million times. Let's
define it:

> Attitude: a state of mind; a position of the body or
> manner of carrying oneself to indicate
> mood.

If you take time to think about why you want a time-
out, or why you don't get a chance to do what you want to
do, you are already beginning to change your attitude.
Changing involves some sort of thinking. When you think
about how you are reacting, how you are feeling, you
start on the road to understanding. When you understand, you become calmer about your situation because
staring anger, rage, and jealousy in the face tends to make
them vanish. You find reasons to change your behavior.
When you decide to change your behavior, to think
more, you have changed your attitude. You become more
positive. Your life will become better. Dr. Bernie Siegel
in his book *Love, Medicine and Miracles* talks about
"attitudinal healing," which is the changing of your attitude toward your life to a positive, constructive one. This
positive attitude heals, according to Dr. Siegel and many
other scientists in the field of medicine. Your mind can
make your life and the lives around you better: healthier
and happier. A healthy mind helps make a healthier
body. The two work together.

Think

Are you jealous of the attention your family members give your physically challenged sibling? Do you feel that you don't have enough time for yourself? Do you *know* that you can control some of your life? You can talk to your family about your sad, mad, angry feelings. Show the love you'd like to have shown to you. Try to change your attitude to one of, "Let's work this out," "Let's try to make each one of us happier." Reading this book shows that you are trying to learn. Thinking about your life is the first step toward a better one. If you choose to improve, if you try hard to understand yourself and others, you are on your way to a happier life. Understanding your feelings frees you! Negative attitudes and feelings use too much of your energy. You can feel exhausted all the time. Save your mind and energy for positive things for yourself and your family members.

Life Skills for Your Future

Changing your attitude about how you treat yourself is something you need to learn to live well for the rest of your life. Your handicapped sibling is not the only difficult person or situation you're going to come across in your lifetime. Our journey through life is not guaranteed to be easy. Things are complicated. But you know your brother or sister. You understand most of what is going on. If you do not understand something, ask. But once you begin to think about your own life, you can understand why you need time for you. If you've been reacting with jealousy, rage, anger, impatience, that's okay. But if you continue simply to react without thinking, you need time-out to think again.

Tips on How to Ask Questions

1. Think first; plan your question. That need not take long—perhaps just the time it takes to breathe deeply twice. Ask yourself: What is my goal? Do I want to get along later? How do I discuss things without making enemies?

2. Try not to blurt out questions or answers to questions. Often the tone of your voice is what others hear, not your words. Slow down and think!

3. If your listener interrupts, ask as calmly as you can to be allowed to finish. Try sitting down if you're not already doing so.

4. If your listener continues to talk, try letting him or her run out of steam. Use the time to think about what you want to say.

5. Speak with love and with a goal of kindness. If you're feeling ugly, say: "I'm feeling ugly." Try not to say in a huff: "I hate you!" If you try to state a fact, not throw a hurtful arrow, you'll have better communication, now and later.

6. If your communication is not going well, *stop!* Ask the person when you can get together again when you both feel like communicating.

7. If you are not coming to an agreement, *stop!* Tell the person kindly that you'll talk later when you've both calmed down. Then be sure to follow up by asking for a specific "talk-time" when you are both calmer.

8. Begin your "talk-time" with your brother, sister, or parent with a statement such as: "I love you and want to get along better," or "I have been feeling sad (or mad or angry) lately, and I would

like your help so we can both live more happily."
9. Notice how your relative looks. Notice his eyes. Look into her face. When you say something nice, notice how he or she looks. You may find the person is happier just hearing beautiful words from you!
10. If words are failing, or tears are falling, try a huge hug!

Be Kind, Act with Love

Have you noticed that all the suggestions in this book have to do with showing kindness and love? You do have control over how you speak to someone if you think a bit before you speak. Sometimes that is very difficult, especially when your physically challenged sibling is in the crabbiest of moods! Or perhaps *you're* not feeling well. Remember one thing: You are not physically challenged. The point is that you must try to understand the sadness and frustration your relative is going through. Since you are not going through the pain, try to treat your sibling with love and understanding—the way you know you'd like to be treated, whether you're handicapped or not.

Should You Let Your Sibling Get Away with Things?

Communicating your feelings does not mean you should be quiet about things that bother you. If you are being treated badly, say something. Try talking it out. Don't let bad behavior continue; it will pile up to a point of anger. Like a splinter under your fingernail, it only bothers you a little at first, but if you don't get it out the damage continues and it becomes extremely painful. Don't accept negative treatment until you can't take another minute of it. Angry outbursts hurt others. Deal with things that truly bother you right away. Try to get agreement on positive, get-along behavior so you all can enjoy your days.

Look Not Down, But Up!

That does not mean that every tiny thing that does not sound perfect to your tired ears must be discussed. People are different. People get sick and tired. That is where your thinking and understanding come in. Try not to take things so seriously that you pick at your family members for every small act. Look toward the lovely, positive things in your morning, the beautiful moments in your afternoons, the happy hours in your evenings. Look not down, but up!

CHAPTER 7

Forgiveness and

Acceptance

By now you should be realizing that this book is a positive one. Even in the face of deep sadness, there is a positive way to look at life. Let's list the stages of grief to make them clear, so we may review and then move forward.

Dr. Elisabeth Kübler-Ross' Stages of Human Grief

1. Denial, avoidance of change
2. Anger, hate, jealousy
3. Bargaining, guilt
4. Depression, overwhelming sadness
5. Acceptance of change, the truth
6. Hope!

Keep Growing, As You Feel

It can't be repeated enough that you are not alone in your very human feelings. The feelings you have are yours.

You are allowed to have feelings. Let yourself have them, feel them, and learn to understand and live with them. But keep growing through them. A healthy person is one who is slowly learning, growing, and changing through life. If you find yourself becoming stuck, seek help. Think, read, write, speak to others, find a way to learn to live well, not just run in place.

Ladasha's father seems to be stuck in the first stage of grief: run away, don't deal with the family problem. Kasib is in the second stage, still hating the situation. Certainly Jeremiah's violent angry feelings tell what stage of grief he is in. Anthony seems to be flowing back and forth from anger and hate, to sadness, to guilt for not wanting to give up a kidney for his brother. Kelsey hates sticks but has resolved not to hate her family members, especially her brother Trevor. She is accepting his situation but has not quite become filled with shining hope—yet. She's still sad about the way life is at times.

It's Okay to Be in More Than One Stage

Learning about the stages of grief should help you understand some of the "crazy-mixed-up" things that go on in your mind and body. However, there is no set time when all of a sudden you move to another stage of grief. And often a person moves in and out of stages, sometimes going back a little to get ahead. Whatever way you are feeling is just that: the way you are feeling. When it hurts your health or the health of others around you it is time to move on, to change or modify your feelings and behavior. Understanding other people's experiences can sometimes help you grow.

Chris

I had a terrible argument with my mother the day she went into the hospital and had my baby sister two months early. I should never have upset her. Now look at what I've done. As I look through the window of the "preemie" intensive care unit, I feel like I'm going to throw up. All I see is a head the size of my hand, a bit of bone and skin, and zillions of needles and tubes sticking out everywhere. We can't see her eyes, because they are taped shut. I just told Mom I was going to the hospital chapel to pray. Maybe if I pray hard enough and long enough and often enough, my baby sister will be able to live. Then I promise to help her learn to walk and talk and to have a good life. I'll help her with everything! I promise.

Demetrius

My sister went blind yesterday and it is all my fault. I had a fight with her about what I don't even remember now. But we were fighting and yelling just before Dad decided to hop in the car to get some ice cream. If Whitney had been playing nicely with me, she wouldn't have wanted to go with Dad, she would have stayed home. And when that drunk driver hit the car, Whitney wouldn't have been in it and the windshield wouldn't have smashed into her eyes and she wouldn't be blind now. Dad's fine. Whitney didn't have her seatbelt on and went flying through the windshield. She has tiny cuts everywhere, but in her eyes those tiny cuts mean blindness. When she comes home from the hospital I am going to be the best older brother you ever saw. I'm going to teach her things and help her get along. No more fighting for us, that's for sure. I'm never fighting with her again.

Who Is to Blame?

Blaming someone for a tragedy does not help anyone. Blame hurts the person who feels guilty and all the people who live with that person. Falling into the "blaming trap" causes hurt so deep that people can actually get sick. Here again, mental attitude can make a person feel well, or feel very ill. Chris and Demetrius have made bargains with God and their families that they will never again fight with their siblings. This bargain is made out of tremendous guilt because they both feel responsible for their sisters' disabilities. The promises are also made because the boys love their sisters. But taking blame, feeling guilty, and making unrealistic promises are not the best ways to show love.

Teach Only Love

Teach Only Love by Dr. Gerald G. Jampolsky is a short easy-to-read book on how to show love. He writes: ". . . the root meaning of the verb *to forgive* is to let go . . . Forgiveness is an inner correction that lightens the heart . . ."

Dr. Jampolsky says that behavior does not even have to change in a certain way, that forgiveness, or understanding your guiltlessness, happens *within* you. When this forgiveness of yourself and others happens, an understanding, a peaceful attitude takes place. This attitude change will heal Chris's stomach upset. A positive, loving change in attitude heals yourself, and that can only help your physically challenged sibling in the end. Your attitude of trying to be positive and showing love will show through in your behavior, and your behavior will help your family members feel more love. Free yourself! Lift

your feelings of guilt! You haven't done anything pur-
posely, you know.

Perhaps Demetrius *will* teach his sister many things
with his love, but he must forgive himself for being
human. To disagree with people helps all of us learn
about our own ideas and others' too. To feel guilt hurts.
Arguing with siblings, family, and friends is healthy. During this family tragedy, love must shine through for you
and your family, not negative feelings that make you sick
inside. Forget the guilt; it does little good to keep it.

Disagreement Is a Normal Part of Growing

Chris and Demetrius are normal people who have fought
and argued with family members. We all argue. The unfortunate thing is that both of them argued the day that a
tremendous tragedy happened in their family. They are
feeling so guilty. Both boys feel as if their siblings' physical challenges are their fault. They feel that if they stop
arguing and pray harder and work harder, the health of
their siblings will improve.

Praying and Hard Work Do Help

It is wonderful that these young people want to make a
good homelife for their sisters. It is beautiful to pray and
work harder to help the family. But it is not healthy for
Chris or Demetrius to keep thinking that an accident or
the early birth of a baby is their fault. Some things in life
can be prevented, and some things just happen. They are
not the fault of anyone. When our lives are touched by a
physical challenge, we have to do the best we can. We
must forgive whoever we think was at fault, even if it
is ourselves. We must forgive ourselves for our human

imperfections. We must begin to see that our lives have changed, and we must do the best with what we do have.

Being Born Challenged Is Just Different

Eric in Chapter 2 is a great example of someone who accepts his sister's physical challenges and treats her like a sister—which is what and who she is. Some say that it's a lot easier to accept a brother or sister who was born before you because he or she has always been there. If a sister or brother has always been physically challenged, the new child born into the family has little to adjust to; that's just the way his sibling is. But sometimes a person born with a physical challenge goes through her grief later, when her life changes in some way.

Courtney

I've been called "handicapped" my entire life. Although I don't feel handicapped, the rest of the world sees me that way. I was born without a left hand and wrist. I have about two thirds of my forearm. I've had a hook-type prosthesis since I was five months old. It is a part of me, and most of the time I don't even think about how I am. I am just me. But lately, I feel some changes going on. I've always had a lot of friends, and I have never had a problem with boys because I have two brothers. I've had eleven years of practice in getting along with them, so I have no trouble talking to guys. Now that I'm in the eighth grade, the idea of dating is becoming quite the subject around the locker room. Many of my friends' parents have allowed them to "date" by going to the movies with a guy. Their parents drop them off and pick them up about a half hour after the movie is over. So basically, my friends date. My parents only allow "group dating" right now—you know, a few girls, a few guys, some of them are couples, some aren't. I have noticed something: I have never been asked out by a guy. Of course, some of my friends haven't been asked either. And most of the time I don't think about my one-handedness, but I'm hoping that that doesn't get in the way of my dating guys . . .

Living with a Loss Is an Up and Down Experience

Acceptance of the change or the physical challenge that has caused grief in your life is the fifth stage in the grief process. If you feel you have accepted your sibling's situation, you're probably growing quite normally. But there may be days when sadness and depression get you into a negative mood again. If that happens to you, it's okay, you're flowing back and forth in the grief process. It doesn't make it easier, but you're going to be fine.

It is a common misunderstanding that people with physical challenges "get over them." As if having a parent die is something you "get over." You don't get over and forget what has happened to you. The experience, the trauma, actually becomes a part of you. You deal with your loss periodically; that is to say, grief comes and goes. In all likelihood it *will* surface again.

Courtney is an excellent example of someone who has been living her life in a positive way, having always accepted her congenital amputation because she has known no other way to live. However, as she grows and matures her life is changing, and she is beginning to think about her physical challenge in a new light. Dating is an issue she had never dealt with before. And this new phase of her life is bringing up different feelings of grief and loss.

Normally very able-bodied, she almost brags about how well she gets along with boys—yet she wonders if any of the guys will ever ask her out. Her physical challenge has become a source of doubt for her. She knows she's different. She wonders how this will affect her dating life.

Courtney's life is not over. *Her* personal grief process may begin at age thirteen. She was born with her challenge, but adolescent change causes doubts. Because the person, the body you used to be in, is changing, Courtney's "born-with acceptance" may fade away for a time. She may begin a grief period she never had before because she's never been a teen before.

If your family has dealt with physical challenge from birth, or for many years, it does not mean that you will always feel comfortable, accepting, or filled with hope. Depression and sadness can arise in anyone at any time. All you need is a trigger, a reminder, to set your mind and heart into sad feelings and thoughts. It is frequently overlooked that a family's long-ago trauma is still difficult to live with. If a family is coping well, outsiders don't even notice what a challenge life can be for those who are physically impaired. If you are growing in a healthy way mentally, you will become sensitive to things now and then that trigger you back into the grief process. Reminders of your loss and your sibling's loss can actually catch you by surprise, like a slap in the face. There may be times when you are fighting or arguing or almost hating your brother or sister, and you're so mixed up you don't know why. Perhaps you are reliving the grief feelings. Even if you're used to your family situation, it can get to you, causing grief.

You Are Not Alone—Ever

One terrific thing about being born an earthling is that we have so many people we can choose to be with, talk to, and seek friendship with. Use the people in your life whom you trust when you find yourself in a moment you simply do not understand. You are never alone! That does not mean that you can't *be* alone. If you want to be alone, to think, to cry, to write, to have a time-out, that is your choice. But when you are frustrated, confused, not yourself, try communicating with your friends and family.

You Will Go Through More Than One Grief

Remember that every one of us goes through strong emotions as we live with changes in our lives. Not every one of us has a personal physical challenge. Not all of us have a disabled sibling. But all of us experience change. And grief over a loss is grief over a major change in our lives. We can help each other through. As life unfolds, as you live through the many phases of your life, one of the things you may have to deal with more than once or twice is the difficult daily challenge of living with a disabled relative. You may go through some of the stages of grief several times in your life. It may not be a comfort to know that life is difficult. But learning about normal feelings helps you to understand yourself. Learning ways to get through difficult challenges will help you grow in healthy, adjusted ways.

You're Okay!

It's okay to feel confused, to feel angry, as if you want to run away. If you put love at the top of your "feelings" list, the other emotions will pass into positive growth. If you act in love *first*, no matter how often you feel anger, or deep sadness, your life will steadily become happier. If you love your brother, if you love your sister, if you love your parents, try your hardest to act with love *first*. It will make a difference in all your lives.

CHAPTER 8

Getting Back
to Living

Since we are beginning to understand the grief process, let us assume that you are somewhere between depression, acceptance of the physical challenge of your brother or sister, and hope. Hope is the final and very positive stage of grief, when you begin to dream again. During these last three stages you should be catching a glimpse of something positive every single day.

Hopeful Ways to Guarantee a Better Day

1. Each day is new; begin it that way. Do not bring any harsh memories over the midnight border to the fresh new morning light. Try to forget the past. Look to the new opportunity to do it all *better* than yesterday—today.

2. *Stop!* Look in the mirror! Find one thing you honestly like about the way you look today. Right now, or any time: Whisper to yourself: "I like my _____."

3. Eat some breakfast. It doesn't have to be much, but have something to get you on your way to a *great day*!
4. Make it a point to say something nice to everyone in your family. Yes, even your brother or sister deserves a great start to the new day.
5. Make a point of *doing* something nice for each person in your family (without bragging or complaining about how much you do for them already . . .). People tend to believe others when words are followed by wonderfully positive *actions*.

André

My three sisters are all older than I am and usually take care of breakfast in the mornings. I'm ten, and I have the trash to collect from every room and also the job of helping my brother change his colostomy bag and get his new one adjusted. He's a paraplegic. He's sixteen and had a tumor removed from his spine. The doctors said it wasn't cancer, which was great, and we were hoping he would be able to keep his lower body working. But during the operation the doctors found more tumor, and more nerve damage happened because they had to get all of the tumor in case it was cancer. We were lucky he didn't die or have to have chemotherapy. Since I'm the only other male in our family besides Dad (who works two jobs now to pay our medical bills), I help my brother get ready for high school every morning. I don't mind. He's my brother. And when I go into his room to help him get cleaned up and ready for school, we hug a lot. Some days, we cry too. But we made a secret pact. We decided that every day we'd go out to the kitchen with smiles on our faces, no matter how hard it was to get him dressed. I take care of the garbage, and he wheels out to the laundry room to start a load of laundry. Then every evening we fold clothes together after they dry during homework time. No matter how sad I get, I make my heart remember that my brother could be dead, but he's alive. And I love him. Mom and I pray together every night before she tucks me in. I miss Daddy since he took that night job, but we're going to be okay. We all have each other, all seven of us.

Special Care Builds a Special Relationship

André's family has a lot of people in it. They're a team. They pull together. They all have jobs, which helps ease the pressure on all of them. Of course, the old saying has a lot of truth in it: Many hands make light work. André does some very mature things for his age. But he has found out that while doing for his family, he has alone time with his brother. They have a special friendship and secret deals. They cry together and hug. They start each day together. In spite of the difficulties, helping a loved one creates a caring time that is yours to share. André does not complain, he *ex*plains his morning. And he has a loving understanding of his brother. André has also realized how breakable life can be. His brother could have died, but he's still around to love.

Try to See the Marvelous Things

The making of lists has true training power. As you write down your positives, you begin to look closely at what is good in your life. That makes you have happier days when you see what you have to smile about. Making daily or weekly lists trains you to think of the successes of your life. All too often we concentrate on the things we don't like about our days. List-making changes your point of view.

Make a Positives-in-My-Life List

Go ahead and try. Every evening before you go to sleep, write in a notebook what you liked about your day. You'll be surprised at how many things have gone well. Write only the positive things. Concentrate on the goodies of your day. Frequently when things are going well we forget the positives. We almost take successful days for granted. List-making gets you into the habit of being thoughtful and thankful for how amazing your life really is. Following are some examples of diary/journal/records of positives.

Jeff's diary:
September 15, 1991
I ate my favorite breakfast food today, french toast. It made my day begin great, because it makes me feel great. I can almost smell the sweet-cinnamony taste now!

Sunday night 10/6/91
I answered all but one of my science test questions correctly—I got a 95!

Wednesday, Oct. 9
My report went very well today; I even made a few of the listeners laugh! That made me feel warm and proud. Afterwards one guy said he had intended to sleep through it, but because I said everything so well he ended up listening and learned a lot. That's *two* things about my report that made me proud of myself.

Friday 11/6/91
That girl I think about a lot smiled right at me today.

Scott's journal:
6/24/91
I *had* to write this down . . . My brother went to the doctor today and found out he only has to wear his scoliosis back-brace eighteen hours a day! That means he can go to school without it!! He still has to sleep in it and wear it all the time at home. Wow! I'm so happy for him! He'll be able to walk the way he'd like and wear shirts instead of sweaters to hide his brace. Since it's summer, that's *super*!

11/26/91
I hugged my brother when I heard his news in June and again today because he's been so happy since he doesn't have to wear the brace to school!

Chelsey's diary:
11/30/91
I had a lot of homework, but I tried to just do it and get it over with, and I did it faster than I ever have before. I'm doing this again.

December 1, 1991, Sunday
Seems like I have time to just sit and think in my room. I like that. Getting my work done instead of hating it really works!

Rob's Recording:
12/2/91
I'm getting excited: Hanukkah has begun! I've been saving for months to give my sister a ticket to a ballet: "The Nutcracker"! Sarah's nine and has epilepsy. She's had some seizures this year because she's growing so fast, and

her medication needs to be readjusted. My parents and Sarah are seeing the doctors every other week to regulate her medicine again. Last year she didn't have any seizures. They're pretty scary. She moves in strange, jerky ways, falls down, and doesn't even remember the seizure. Except that she is so exhausted she feels like spaghetti— she says that's how she knows she's had a seizure, but she does not remember a thing about them. I've learned how to help her. I'm twelve and have had to help her many times. I sit on the floor and cradle her head in my lap, turning it to one side, so she doesn't hurt herself and her tongue doesn't fall back down her throat. She could suffocate if that happened. Anyway . . . my sister takes ballet and is a beautiful dancer. She's never been to a real ballet on stage, so I bought her a ticket with my own money. Mom and Dad are going to buy the other tickets and we're all going on the last night of Hanukkah. What a holiday this is going to be! She'll be so surprised. She doesn't know it, but I'm saving her best present for *last*! A Hanukkah to remember!

12/13/91

Sarah cried happy tears when she opened the envelope with her ballet ticket. "The Nutcracker" was unbelievable! I think Sarah wants to be a professional ballet dancer now, she had such a great time. It was worth it to save up for the best box seats. She said she felt like a princess. I'll never forget how happy I was *this* Hanukkah!

Dream a Dream for You

Now that you have thought about—or just tried to think about—the positive things in your life, you're ready for the next step. At night, before you drift off to sleep, try visualizing yourself where you'd love to be. Create a movie in your mind. Some nights you may get only as far as a minute or two. That's fine. The fun part of this exercise is *trying* to dream. If you do this for a week, you'll find that you will begin to train yourself to dream. And often, if you continue your "movie of the mind," focusing on seeing yourself where you'd like to be, the dreams you dream will take you there. Scientists, behavioral psychologists, and psychiatrists have studied dream patterns for decades. In many books on dreams, some based on Edgar Cayce's work on the mind and soul, it is suggested that through journal-writing we can pattern our dreams and also remember them. More about this in Chapter 12 on journal-writing. For now, try to get going by choosing what you'd like to dream about. If you have ever been in love you'll identify with the next person's story.

Juan

The minute I saw her I felt my heart jump in place. Not only do I like the way she looks and her long, wavy black hair, but Francesca moves as if she knows herself. She knows what she wants and goes about getting it. She is not a natural student—you know, the type who can get an A with her eyes closed. No, Francesca studies for her As, and she gets almost all 90s on her work. She also likes clothes. So even though she's a full-time senior in high school, she has a thirty-hour-a-week job at a department store. She sells more than anyone in her department. She's intelligent. She not only works hard and well, so they give her as many hours as she can handle, but she also receives a discount on clothes. Smart! Some days I lie awake at night and think of her smile. Ever since I saw her four weeks ago I've been having dreams about her too! I dream we date, we go swimming, or we work together in the same store. One morning I didn't want to open my eyes because Francesca and I were in Hawaii! She is all I think about besides getting my schoolwork done. Sometimes it's hard to focus on that too, since I daydream about her a lot. We had lunch at the same table yesterday. Replaying that will probably give me enough to dream about for two weeks!

It Is Natural to Dream

Dreaming is as natural as rain. While our bodies are relaxing, our minds are free to think and do. That has been a problem for many a teacher—students who daydream in class are not listening with all of their abilities, are they? But daydreaming can be a wonderful escape when we're doing something boring such as folding clothes or riding a bus.

Learning to dream and giving yourself permission to dream is a new, enjoyable, and private thing to do for *yourself*. After reading Juan's story, you probably know how to program yourself to dream. Let yourself go!

Dream Topics to Try

- See yourself as an adult. What would you like to be? What career?
- You have the entire night ahead to dream—where do you want to travel?
- Picture your physically challenged sibling well again—what would you want to do with him or her?
- If you had one wish, what would it be? Go ahead and wish it now: in detail and in color.

- If you're hungry, what foods would you like to see on a huge tray on top of your bed? See yourself tasting, smelling, and enjoying.
- Now that you've been dreaming, some may be a little unrealistic—which is terrific! Now try a realistic dream—a "you-can-do-it" dream.

Set Up a System

When you have had some wonderful dreams, you've tasted some fun, even excitement at the possibility of some of your dreams. Now it is time to talk again with your family: with your parents and caregivers. After dreamtime, after the excitement of perhaps having a wonderfully different life, you have some special energy inside. Use that energy! Express your feelings to your parents. Ask for a time to talk seriously about *you*. Explain that you give special time to your disabled sibling, and now you'd like to spend special time with your parents. Set a time. No television, no stereo, just you and your parents, perhaps a snack and a drink, but no one else.

Plan for your appointment with your parents. Write down a few of your realistic dreams, the ones that are most important to you. Then talk to them about setting up a system under which you do for the family and then have time to accomplish things for yourself. Planning the steps to achieve personal goals and dreams helps to make those goals and dreams come true. If a dream of yours can actually come true, you should be able to talk it over with your parents so you may touch that dream. Many dreams take money to realize, so perhaps you'll have to learn to budget your money and set up a savings plan. Listen to your parents as they set up a schedule or suggest ideas.

They can help you reach your dream if you give them your best listening power. Let your mind be open and free to learn.

Jenna

One night I had a dream, I couldn't have planned better! I dreamed I became a prosthetist. That's someone who makes the artificial arms, hands, legs, and feet for amputees. My older brother Trey is an amputee. He and his friends were out drinking beer one night and boom, had an unbelievable accident. No one died, but Trey's arm was cut off by a flying piece of metal from the car door that had been ripped off. The driver was speeding on a local road we all know has a dangerous bend. That didn't matter to him. He just sped along, not a care in the world . . . I hate what happened to Trey. He's twenty now and a sophomore at Tech. He's still on the basketball team wherever he goes; he just has to play a lot differently than before his accident three years ago. I'm graduating from high school next year and have had a hard time with Trey's accident. The two of us have been so athletic and on every ball team around. I mean, I am not only a cheerleader, but run distance on the track team and play softball all summer long. Trey was on the football, basketball, and baseball teams for as long as I can remember. This is the first team he's been able to play on for three years, and has he been happy since the basketball season began! Anyway. I've been trying to get happier, thinking of dreams I'd like to see for myself, and all of a sudden one night I dreamed I was a prosthetist! The day before my dream, we had all gone (Mom, Dad, Trey, and me) to get Trey's myoelectronic, five-fingered hand and arm repaired. He fell on it during the last basketball game and broke the thumb half-way off. Anyway, it makes total sense for me to think about going to college to learn to make prostheses. I love science, and you have to study the body—especially the bones and muscle structure—to become a prosthetist. Also, I already understand how the patients feel about losing a part of their body. I've cried with my brother for three years now. The idea in this dream made me so happy, I couldn't wait to tell my parents. Right now we have a plan. I'm going to write to all the colleges that have prosthetic departments and see what their requirements are. I haven't been accepted yet, but it's a start. I can always spend double time improving my grades, if I need to. That dream has given me a real goal I can get excited about. Maybe I'll invent the best prosthesis Trey ever had. He can be my special project in school: making a prosthesis that can best help the basketball player perform! Paralympics here we come!

Make Use of Your Experience

It is interesting that Jenna's dream has actually changed her life. She was trying to make her life happier by the dream suggestions we've talked about. But in the process she dreamed an "unplanned dream" that has made her happier and has molded the direction of her life.

Your Mind Can Set You Free!

You may have felt very trapped in your family situation. Let's now assume that you are through your grief for a while. You've accepted your family situation, and you help your family on a daily basis with a system. That is to say, you and your family have figured out a way to share the work involved in caring for your physically challenged brother/sister. You've sat down together and planned free time for everyone too. Now you are trying to use some of that free time you hadn't planned on before your "system." Well, let your mind free your life. Now is the time to convince your family that some of your dreams need to come true so you can feel strong and more like you.

Luke

> My life has been
> About my Dad
> He's meant so much to me.
> But now I'm older
> And life is harsher
> I don't want to be colder,
> I just want to be me.

Luke has a wonderful dad, who is his hero. But Luke is coming to the age when he wants to deal with the difficulties of life, yet he doesn't want to grow mean and cold and uncaring. If you decide you *don't* want to be a certain way, that's great! In all of this decision-making, the process may actually be the opposite of what you think developing "your own you" is all about. Frequently we make decisions by finding out what we *do not* like. In that way, you are still closing in on how you feel, but not by saying yes as much as by saying no!

Taking care of a physically challenged sibling forces you to think of others. Good. It may also push you to decide that certain things will *not* be part of your life. That is good development too. But don't decide these things with anger, letting yourself "suffer silently" until you're eighteen and go out on your own. Discuss your feelings with your family. As you grow older, you want to be more independent of your parents. Work with them so that you don't become cold and angry because you don't see your life the way you'd like. You have the controls here; talk it out.

Rotate or Change the System

If you have been working with a family system under which everyone has a part in the care of the house, the meals, the laundry, and the care of one another, that's great. Now make life interesting by rotating some or all of the chores. And remember that the physically challenged person must participate in the family system; she's a member of the family, isn't she?

Try making a chart on posterboard. For fifty cents, you have two sides for two separate switch-the-system charts.

Notice that no one has more than one or two things to

Jobs*	Mon.	Tues.	Wed.	Thurs.	Fri.	Sat.	Sun.
Family Work Schedule							
1 load laundry (wash, dry, fold)	T	S		M	D	M	
Vacuum house		T			S		
Dust house			T				
Make Dinner	M	D	S	T	M	D	M
Put away clean dishes	D	M	D	S	T	S	T
Take out all garbage	S			T			
Clean bathrooms		S				T	

* Everyone makes his/her own bed and keeps room clean, picks up after eating or drinking anything!
T = Theo   S = Shaheeda   M = Mom   D = Dad

do on any day. This is a sample chart, so a few of the things you need to get done at home may have to be added to the job list. You will begin to realize what you've missed when things are not getting done by anyone. If you discuss this in a family meeting, perhaps you can also emphasize that if everyone picked up after himself, the house would only need attention on deep-cleaning days.

Notice also the suggestion to do a load of laundry almost every day. That prevents the depressing occurrence of a *huge* "laundry day." Keeping ahead of laundry is a big problem in running a household, especially if there is a bedridden member. Sheets and towels may fill up a washer, and your favorite jeans don't make it. Thinking of chores as necessary, but movable, tradeable jobs can make them less dreaded. A side effect of scheduling jobs is cutting down on yelling and screaming. All a member has to do is check the chart and do his job.

Now You Have Even More Free Time

After you've discussed and planned for shared family responsibilities, you'll find that you have more time. Schedules can be switched around so that you are not a slave to your home and your siblings. Even though your life has been changed by disability, you still have time. Pick a dream of yours, and take a step toward that dream. If you want to go to college to pursue a certain career, like Jenna, go to the library and begin learning more about your special dream. If you have extra money, buy some special materials on your favorite subjects. Jenna could arrange to be an apprentice at a local prosthetic business, perhaps the one that her family uses for her brother's prostheses. She could start learning now; why wait until college?

Hobbies

If you can't think of a thing to do, try something absolutely and entirely new. The word hobby may not be one you are familiar with:

> Hobby: a pursuit outside one's regular occupation,
> engaged in for relaxation.

Your occupation may be part-time job and full-time student at the moment, so a hobby may be all the other things you don't do while you're busy working and studying: fishing, making Christmas gifts, biking, hiking, studying animals, snakes, leaves, trees, other plants, scouts, youth group, etc . . .

Your Life Can Be Your Own

You *can* begin to live again. You can be in charge of some of your time. Actually, if you take time to communicate with your family, to explain that at times you feel overwhelmed with your sibling's physical challenges, you're already beginning to take charge of your time. When you're successful in making a better environment for yourself and each of your relatives, it makes your life more your own.

CHAPTER 9

Sharing

L earning is an up and down experience, a curve that can go on for the rest of your life, or you can get stuck in a phase or a stage of grief while you are figuring out how you feel and which way to turn.

When there is a disability in a family, communicating with family members is not always easy. It takes extra effort and gentler ways to talk with your family. As has been discussed in previous chapters, your *timing* and your *approach* can make all the difference. It's like trying to talk to your mother when the television is blaring or someone walks in with a boombox screaming. The chances are slim of her actually blocking out everything else to hear what you're saying. Mom has a lot on her mind too. If you've had trouble relaying your messages-from-the-heart, try again.

Can Family Members Be Too Close?

Frustrating as it is to signal to people that something is wrong, sometimes family members are too close. There is an old saying: "You can't see the forest for the trees."

Often when a difficult experience is happening in a family, the members are too involved in their own drama to see "the whole picture." In other words, they see only the few trees around them and not the entire forest. It is time then to seek a friend or a trusted person with whom to share your experience. Getting a new point of view can enable you to see another side of your problems, help you see the complete picture.

Even if you do communicate well with your family members, there may be feelings you have put in your journal, or thoughts you've had, that are still foggy and unclear. Choosing to discuss your thoughts and concerns with others can make all the difference in how you see yourself. Sharing with another person can make that crystal clear.

Katelyn

I was sitting in church while the pastor was speaking yesterday when I just started crying. I know it was only a few tears, but what he was saying hit home: "If you aren't sure you're happy, talk to someone about how you are feeling." I quickly grabbed a tissue and pretended I just had to blow my nose. I didn't want everyone to see me upset, or they'd all ask what was wrong. After the service my Sunday School teacher came over and gave me a big hug and walked me to class. That did it again. I began crying. She led me to the ladies' room, where she got a cold wet towel and cooled my burning face. I told her I didn't *know* what was the matter, I just wanted to cry. We agreed to meet after class, and she said she'd ask Mom if she could take me to lunch. I feel great already! Just knowing I have someone to cry with makes me feel relief. I'm trying to be good and do everything right at home while my sister Kara is getting IV antibiotics to fight a huge infection she has because of her leukemia. But sometimes it all just gets to me. I do talk about my sister to Mom. I keep my diary every night. I have so many, many feelings. I'm scared. I don't want my sister to die . . .

People Need People

People *do* need people. You need yourself, and you must learn to be independent and think for yourself. But we're placed on this wonderful planet with millions of other people. We should think about using those people—meaning, let's share our talents, share our need to be cared for by each other. Katelyn is hurting. Her family has been going through much pain because of Kara's leukemia. Life is a burden when it is so uncertain. Katelyn already feels relief with just the thought that she has someone with whom to share it. What a difference an hour with a trusted friend can make for your spirits!

Make Another Positive-Attitude List!

Try making a list of all the people you care for, with whom you have shared something before—people you've found to be trustworthy and private. You want your personal thoughts to be just that—personal. People who do not keep your affairs to themselves are not people with whom you should share your deepest thoughts. You have enough to figure out, enough to straighten out without someone gossiping or spreading personal information about you. In choosing a confidant, a person to share your pain, try to choose wisely.

People-to-Talk-with List

1. Brother or sister
2. Parents
3. Best friend
4. 2nd best friend
5. Friend of the opposite sex
6. School counselor
7. Favorite teacher
8. Another favorite teacher
9. Church youth group leader
10. Church leader
11. Neighbor
12. Athletic coach
13. Music director
14. The new kid at school (could use a friend and be one too)
15. Your doctor, nurse, etc.

You're the Manager of Your Own Health

If you don't already drive, you at least know what a backseat driver is. Take the wheel and steer your own life. Start sharing your thoughts with people, your special chosen few. Help them learn about your situation a little bit. Sharing your feelings will make you happier and more free. During the sharing, you may get a clearer picture of how you feel. You may find that some of your feelings are not simply because you have a physically challenged sibling, but because you're a human being. Stay in good health with good life skills. And an excellent life skill to have is creating positive, healthy relationships. Let's face it, you'll be living and dealing with people throughout your life. Even though you have gone through some terrible times, so have others. If you share your thoughts, put into words how you feel, you'll find you're not the only one struggling.

But what about the one who does not know how to be a friend?

Griff

I talked to this guy on my football team about my brother, who has muscular dystrophy. See, Clay has always had this muscle disease. He was born with it. But now that he's fifteen and his body is changing as he becomes a man, his muscles are slowly weakening. It is so hard to see my friend and brother like this. He used to be able to walk with only braces, but now he has to use crutches. I'm afraid if this keeps getting worse he'll have to live in a wheelchair. I know he doesn't want that. And here I am playing senior-high football. It isn't fair, you know? Anyway, I told Jake about Clay and how he's getting worse. I found out this morning that Jake went and told everybody I was having a mental breakdown because as I talked to him tears filled my eyes. I am now so embarrassed I can't see straight. Really, all I want to do is look at the floor as I walk through the halls. One guy on the team actually asked me if I was going to cry during practice today. I don't know who to trust any more.

Griff needs some other help, specifically from someone in the school. This is when a professional is needed. Even if Griff has never talked to the guidance counselor before, he should go now. Things are out of his control because his "friend" decided to make fun of him rather than respect his feelings. Griff is going through even more sadness now and needs the help of someone who he knows will not "spread it around." Griff could ask a teacher he likes to help him set up seeing the counselor. It is part of every teacher's job to help you get help. A sensitive teacher will ask if there's anything wrong even before you ask her. But Griff can't wait for someone to notice that he's having difficulties.

Everyone has problems of his own and may not be alert enough to see your sadness. Do not wait when you are hurting—tell someone. If that person doesn't listen or respond, speak to someone else. School or church people are specially trained to listen. Be sure you say enough, however, because most of us have not been trained to read minds. We have our own lives, and try as we may, we educators can overlook people's concerns.

Write a Note

Try writing a note if you feel so uncomfortable about your family challenges that you don't want to cause a scene. Teachers, coaches, and guidance counselors do not mind if you cry, but chances are you'd mind. So write a note to your favorite adult asking for time to talk, or even stating what has happened that is making you sad. This is a simple and effective tool of communication. You can leave notes to apologize, to thank people, and to explain what you are going through. Notes are a way to reach out to others. Being close to someone during stress is important to your own health and well-being.

Write a Letter

Do you have a friend to whom you can write a letter? Perhaps you've moved and miss sharing things with a special friend. Go ahead and write a letter explaining your situation. Ask him or her to write back, or perhaps give you a call.

You may even want to write to an aunt, an uncle, or a cousin who lives too far away to see very much. Try writing a letter with honest statements about your family situation. Don't write anything hateful. Concentrate on your own reactions and sadness about how *you're* feeling, taking part in a physically challenged person's life, how things look to you. Getting another person's opinion can make your days much brighter. An outside point of view allows you to see the entire forest. Your challenges may seem as big as the tallest redwood, but you are okay, and the forest is still very green and alive. In the big picture, you are going to get through, if you try.

Don't Leave Out Your Sibling

Sometimes the one who seemingly is the source of your trouble, your pain, is the one you should turn to for help and understanding. Have you tried seeing your sibling as someone who may understand *your* feelings?

James

I have spent the last twelve years, which is all of my age, asking my brother Antoine if he is all right. I worry about him so much. He has cystic fibrosis and usually goes into the hospital twice a year to clear his lungs and help him fight the continual chest infections he gets because of his trouble breathing. Lately, I've been fighting with him. I seem to yell at him. When we play games, I scream at him if he says he's tired. Antoine is fifteen, but this past summer I grew an inch, so now I'm taller than he is. I'm changing. I know I love my brother, so why do I yell at him or have so little patience? Right now he's going through a bad period of breathing. He uses a portable breathing machine every night before bed. I know his cystic fibrosis pattern: Soon my parents will have to take him to the hospital if his breathing gets more labored. Antoine's lungs fill with fluid, which can then get infected if he can't cough it out. He's actually glad when he goes to the hospital, because with breathing help twenty-four hours a day he gets to feeling super. When he comes home he is usually flying high, feeling so fresh, so able to breathe. I can't understand how I can be so mean to him after all he goes through.

James seems to want to apologize for his behavior to Antoine, yet he doesn't have a real reason why he's acting so negatively. Perhaps the best way to deal with his "unknowns" is to talk it out with the person he's treating so badly: his brother. If you argue with someone, deal with that someone. You can prevent all sorts of other problems if you catch the problem at the beginning.

Face Your Fears

How do you face your fears? The simplest way is just to do it. Talk to the person with whom you're having uneasiness. James should explain to Antoine exactly what he has said—that he does not know why he's acting this way. Sharing your thoughts with the person shows your concern and that you take responsibility for your own actions. Simply explain that you're not out to hurt, that you are confused. Try! Your sibling knows the most about your whole situation; sometimes he or she knows more than your parents do.

Antoine

James, I am so glad you told me you really aren't mad at me! I was beginning to think I was doing everything wrong lately. I don't want to hurt you either. You're my brother, my closest friend! Who else would put up with all the aggravation that goes into getting me to just *breathe*? I mean some days I wish I could run away from this cystic fibrosis to a body store and buy a new body. But I can't. And I guess you probably have had that wish too, especially since I am having such a sick spell. But you can't buy a new brother, can you? What should we do so we don't get on each other's nerves?

CHAPTER 10

Becoming Genuinely Involved

What should you do so that you and your sibling don't get on each other's nerves? Have you asked about anything besides his or her physical condition lately? Behind that physically challenged body is an extra special human being. Have you taken time to get to know the other parts of your sibling's personality? Or are you looking only at his physical challenge, like most of the rest of the world . . .

Rebecca

I asked my sister why she was staying in her room so long. I hadn't thought much about the personal part of my ten-year-old sister before. She's a just a kid, right? She was born with a curved spine that gradually grew worse, so she had surgery and now has to were a backbrace-vest for the next couple of years. We have all been concentrating on getting her through the surgery, recovering from that, and then fitting her with the brace. Now we're trying to persuade her to stay positive, to cooperate and follow her doctor's instructions to wear the brace at least twelve hours daily. I hadn't even thought she might be interested in guys. Tonight when I asked her why she was in her room so long, she just started crying. Then she told me she has fallen for this guy Kyle who goes to our church and is also in her math class. Since math is Allyson's favorite subject, she knows Kyle thinks she's smart. But today because she had a lot of pain she didn't concentrate and failed her math test. Now she's worried that Kyle will find out and not like her. My little sister is growing up! And now maybe I can help her because I can finally identify with her. She doesn't seem like such a little kid any more. She's a teenager like me! I've decided to surprise her and get permission from Dad to take her, Kyle, a couple of her other friends, and my boyfriend to the movies. We'll fill up the van and then go for ice cream afterward. Dad won't think it's a "date" because it's a whole group of us, but to Allyson it will be. That'll make her feel great.

Tunnel Vision

We all have periods in our lives when we deal with experiences so intense that we tend to forget the rest of the world. That's a kind of tunnel vision. Rebecca has been experiencing this as she went through a traumatic year of surgery for her sister. This is normal when you are struggling through such personal pain. You don't even have enough energy for your own troubles, and when you add a physically challenged sibling to worry about, tunnel vision has to set in. It is a form of survival. But sisters keep maturing, in spite of their physical challenges. Poor

Allyson! Her personal development has not been on hold through this year, but sixteen-year-old Rebecca has not noticed.

Rebecca now has the right idea, even though she figured it out quite by accident. She loves her sister and happened to ask her a personal question. Sometimes that's all it takes: asking your family member a personal question instead of "How's your back?" Try to put yourself into your sibling's shoes. How would you be feeling about dating? How would you be feeling about clothes if you had to wear a full chest/backbrace vest? Try to identify with your brother or sister on a personal, close-friend level. You may find there is much more that you love about her besides her strength!

Become Part of Your Sibling's Medical Team

Part of the reason James is treating Antoine badly is fear. James may be afraid for Antoine, and even for himself. What is life, when it can be so difficult, so uncertain? If Antoine cannot breathe, he may die. Death is a very real fear, and James's family deals with that fear more than once every year. Illness and the fear of what illness could bring to a family is scary.

Listening Is Half of Communication

A positive and personal involvement in your physically challenged sibling's life could be a decision to learn more about his condition. Understanding as much as possible can make you feel more at ease. Understanding the treatment can also eliminate fears. Go to the next appointment with your brother or sister. Even if you have to take time off from school or your job, decide to make a trip with your sibling to his or her next medical appointment. Prepare yourself a little bit first:

1. Make a list of questions on your sibling's condition. Keep the list handy so you can add questions as you think of them.
2. Before going to the appointment, ask your sibling your questions. You may be surprised how much he or she knows.
3. Plan with your parent or whoever is taking you to the appointment to have lunch or a special treat as part of the day. There's nothing wrong with making appointments pleasant!
4. Begin the medical appointment by *listening*. Some of your questions may be answered during the examination and visit.
5. Respect your sibling's wishes about privacy if the exam involves exposure of private areas of the body.
6. After the exam it is time to ask your questions. Do not be afraid of your medical team members. Your family are paying for the medical advice of the people who examine your sibling. Take notes if something important or new is said.
7. Discuss any new information with your family members. Come to a complete understanding on treatment. Make a plan of support for your sibling's health, with his or her opinions and wishes respected.
8. Treat this newfound understanding with care. Treat your sibling as you would want to be treated.
9. Notice that your anger or your fears have dissolved. Knowing is learning. Learning paves the

way to understanding. If you understand someone's point of view, you are more apt to treat him
or her with care rather than anger.
10. Enjoy your new relationship with your brother
or sister. By this time you're sure to notice that
your sibling has begun to smile and share with
you more because you're showing a new interest.

Learn for Yourself Too!

The valuable lesson to learn from your medical involvement with your sibling is that you are part of a medical
team. This is an excellent attitude to adopt whenever you
have a medical appointment. You are the manager of your
own health. You can make a list of questions, ask them,
and get information so that if something goes wrong you
will know enough about your own health and treatment
not to be afraid, but to cooperate with your medical
team. Learning to manage your body means you'll remain
healthy for a long, long time.

More Fun to Come!

It is hoped that by this time you have also learned a lot
about your brother or sister and have found more to love
about him or her. Have some fun with this friend. Think
of things to do that have nothing to do with the physical
challenge. Of course, you may think ahead about meeting
the physical needs of your sibling, but that can be done
without a big discussion. If walking is a problem and you
are going to a new place, for instance, telephone ahead to
find out about ramps, entrances, and parking. But try to
focus on the fun rather than any special effort that has to
be made. Look into plays, ballgames, shows that cost

little or nothing but are new to both of you. Schools and colleges have performances of all kinds. Go to a museum, library, or park that you rarely visit. The point is to discuss, plan, and actually *do* things with your brother or sister that are just fun. You'll find that you have more in common if you experience more things together.

CHAPTER 11

Dating: Special Time with Your Parents

n Chapter 4 we mentioned the idea of spending time with your parents, personal alone-time. As you have read along, more hints have been given that it is valuable to plan personal time with your caregivers. Whether you are in a foster home, with natural parents, or with adoptive parents, you are with people who care about you. This chapter will try to convince you, with many suggestions, that it is important to enjoy time with your parents. Showing that you care, sharing fun, can refresh and renew what may have been questioned because of personal tragedy. No matter how difficult times have been, they still care.

The Healing Partnership

Dr. Siegel writes in *Love, Medicine and Miracles* of a healing partnership. He also writes: "One of the best ways to make something happen is to predict it." Dr. Siegel has based his books on cancer patient research, but all human patterns of grief are the same. We all seem to have the same reactions to huge and unplanned changes in our lives. Dr. Siegel urges keeping an open mind if you want to feel better, to be healed. In other words, don't conclude that because of the physical challenges in your family you'll never have a life of your own. Rather, predict to yourself and to others that we'll be all right, we'll be well again. Predict success every day, and you'll live to see your own success and that of your family and friends too.

It's in Your Trust and Attitude

You have control over your thoughts. Don't play victim, don't say: "I can't do anything about this or that . . ." Decide that you want to have a healing partnership with the people around you. If you think, "This is going to be a bad day" or "My parents are not going to listen to me," in all likelihood that will be true. You may even think you have had nothing to do with it, but you have. If, however, you have faith that all things have some good in them, you'll begin to see the good because you're looking for it. You think your family life is difficult and certainly not like everyone else's, but how do you know? Every family has its own troubles. Wondering why your situation is the worst wastes a lot of time concentrating on negatives.

Derrick

My brother Chad has cerebral palsy. He has very little control of his hand, arm, and head movements. He's sixteen now, and boy is he smart! He was born with the palsy and has gradually become weaker. But he gets straight As no matter what course he takes at school. He's a poet and one of the funniest people I know. I love him!

The other day I was thinking about my friend Craig, who always seems so together. He has a great girlfriend and is smart and popular and an excellent trumpet player in the All-Star Band. I was thinking I sure would like to be in his shoes. Then yesterday I found out his parents are getting a divorce. Craig doesn't have a brother to talk to about it, so he was telling me in the locker-room before gym. He was crying and saying he didn't see how he could choose whether to live with his mother or his father, he loved them both so much. As I walked home I felt pretty good about *my* parents, who never go a day without kissing each other, and *my* brother, when Craig has no brother at all.

Be Thankful for What You Have

Healing partnerships begin with *knowing* that you have people and situations around you that you like and appreciate. Write down ten things for which you are thankful.

Ten People or Things for Which I Am Grateful	
1. My father	6. My own bedroom
2. My mother	7. My own bed
3. My brother	8. My neighborhood
4. My sister	9. My friend
5. My cat	10. My minister, priest, rabbi

Try not to list "purchased items" so much as people and situations that have been a part of your life.

Now of the people listed give two reasons why you listed them.

Examples:

1. My father: He makes me laugh, he teaches me things.
2. My mother: She loves me, she makes me study or I'd be really lazy.
3. My brother: He shares stuff with me, he teaches me patience because he is patient.
4. My sister: She always knows what I mean, she has fun girlfriends.
5. My cat: She is so soft, she notices me.

Focus on Parents

Now focus: Make a close-up picture in your mind of your parents. What did you list about them? List two more things that you love about them.

My Father	My Mother
• makes me laugh	• loves me
• teaches me things	• makes me not be lazy
• his hugs are HUGE	• her hugs are sweet and cuddly
• expects me to do well, so I usually do	• worries about me, which shows she cares

Take What You've Written and Use It

The next step is to remember the loving things you have listed about your parents and share them. Ask for a "date" with one or both of your parents, and make it a point to compliment them on the things you like and love about your life with them. You don't have to make a speech; simply tell them why you love them. You'll be surprised at their reaction; they'll most likely tell you a few things that will make you smile! Smiles and laughter make people happy. Happier people have better relationships, better partnerships in life. You can do it!

Parent Date

Try a few of these sharing suggestions, some of which have already been mentioned in other chapters:

- Communicate—ask for alone-time with your parent.
- Write a note just to say you care, or make a friendly card with a joke to lighten the moment.
- Plan a surprise night out, perhaps to a movie, or save money to take them out for ice cream or whatever.
- Set up a game and leave it in place until your parent has time to play.
- Write a letter and mail it to your parent at work, requesting an appointment for fun, or telling about your most recent personal joy.
- Show an interest in your parent's interests: Suggest going to work with your parent for half a day, ending with lunch out; or take lunch and have a picnic in the middle of a workday.
- Write your next assignment as a creative story about your parents. Write positive, terrific things about them, and frame the final copy to give to them.
- Just before bed, tell them you care.

CHAPTER 12

Keep a Record
of Your Life

Depending on your experience, you may think a diary is a great way to save personal secrets, or something only little children do. Yes and no. Diaries are very personal. But journals have been kept by *adults* since the earliest records found. Diaries, journals, and records of people's lives have often been the way we have learned how people in our own history have lived. Many adults wrote down their tales of hardship and joy as they settled new territories in Colonial days. There were no newspapers, no systematic mail services. Communication with people was scant. It was a comfort to talk to others (or even to oneself!) in a diary.

Why, then, keep a journal now, when we can just pick up a telephone or go to a friend's house and talk her ears off?

Do you tell your innermost feelings? Most of us are not talkative enough to tell all of what we're experiencing, perhaps partly because we don't *know* how we're feeling.

We haven't defined what's up. Most of us talk to others about the events of recent days and personalities. Only close personal friends tell of the inner sadness they feel from time to time.

Keeping a record of your feelings on a daily, weekly, or monthly basis can help you understand yourself. Writing or drawing in a journal is having a talk with yourself. No matter how you may feel about your family or friends, you can always count on your "self." You are you, and if you understand yourself you can be your own best friend. That can be a true comfort, especially as you encounter new situations when you don't know anyone and feel alone. Being by yourself is not bad. You are never totally alone; you have *you* to count on—always!

Some people think writing a diary is almost like talking out loud to yourself. It is, but not in a negative way. People make fun of those who mumble to themselves. How do you know whether people whose mouths are moving as they drive along are singing along with the radio or talking to themselves? Isn't singing a form of talking to yourself? What's wrong with that? Not a thing!

Taking an active role in knowing and understanding yourself is a positive way to live. This chapter gives examples of many forms of recording your life. When you are older, even only a year older, you will be able to look back and see how you've grown. Watching yourself grow is rewarding because you realize how far you've come.

The Record of Your Life

Chances are you are already keeping a record of your life, or perhaps your parents are doing it, in the form of photographs. Baby pictures, "your first step," that lost baby-tooth that's tucked away in your parent's drawer, are all records of your development. A personal record of your life is basically a scrapbook of memories. You can write, draw, or paste in photographs, pictures from magazines, articles from newspapers on your accomplishments—you name it, it is your life! Keeping a record need not take a lot of time. Look at the following journal entries, and see how long it would take to write one per day:

Lindsey

1/11/90 I made the cheerleading squad! I feel FABULOUS!

1/14/90 I'm exhausted from practice, but I love being out in front of everyone at the games.

1/16/90 We lost again, that makes four out of four. I feel bad for the team, but I'm having a great time anyway . . .

3/5/90 Today was our last game and end-of-the-season party. What a blast! I'll never forget Jay's face when he was hit in the face with that pie. I'm going to miss cheering . . .

4/30/90 I'm pasting photos of the squad and end-of-season bash in the pages following.

Parker

12.4.91 My brother got hit by a truck. All I want to do is cry.

12.5.91 When I saw my big brother he was full of blood. A piece of metal had cut his throat. He's got a broken leg, and he can't talk.

12.6.91   I wonder if Cliff will be home for Christmas. I don't want to have Christmas at all. Not without him.

12.7.91   The doctors say Cliff might not be able to talk if the cuts on his voicebox heal with much scar tissue. All I want to do is cry.

12.8.91   I can't do any homework. Cliff's still not home.

12.9.91   Cliff writes us notes when we go to see him at the hospital. It's so sad. I hate this.

12.10.91   Dad came in my room just now. He said they sent for a speech therapist who knows sign language to begin teaching Cliff while he's still in the hospital. Dad said it's just in case Cliff can't talk for longer than they figured. I feel like it's raining inside my head. Tears, tears, tears . . .

12.11.91   Today I felt so bad, I told Mom I couldn't go to school. Why did this happen to him; why not me?

12.12.91   Yesterday Mom surprised me by taking the day off too. We stayed with Cliff all day. I learned "Hi" in sign language, even though I know Cliff can hear me. I want to learn so he can't get away with saying stuff I don't understand. Big brothers do that, especially when they're only a year older. . . . I miss the old Cliff.

12.13.91   *Cliff's home*!!!!!!!!!!!!!!!!!!!!!!!!!! I put a dead spider on his pillow just so he knows I was thinking of him. He laughed, but no sound came out. I'm happy he's home, but all I can do is run to my room, cry, and talk to my journal . . .

12.15.91   It's so quiet in this house I want to scream.

12.19.91   Trucks suck.

12.20.91 Every time I see a truck, I see Cliff being hit. I even had a dream about the accident last night.

12.24.91 Tomorrow's Christmas. Cliff doesn't have any more stitches, no more bandages, just his cast. He still can't speak. We just don't know. But it is the *best Christmas of my life* because my brother's still alive. Sad or not, it's the best Christmas ever.

Short, but Maybe Not Sweet

Pasting pictures, news articles, paper napkins, and other memorabilia in your journal/scrapbook takes a minute or two. Jotting down a thought takes even less time. Try it! As you can see, Parker sometimes only had two words to say, or a phrase to blurt out on paper. Although swearing is not acceptable language, at times writing down an ugly word can get your anger out. It's safer than swearing, which can get you grounded, suspended, or otherwise ousted. But what you write in your journal is a private affair. You may choose to share some or all of the pages with a buddy or a special someone, but you have the right not to share your record with anyone. Write short sentences of anger, or long paragraphs of phrases. There are no rules, no grammar tests or spelling needs here. Just say it so you can eventually figure yourself out. Write it to relieve the pain, or to spread your pages with joy.

Figure Them Out

In reading Lindsey's and Parker's journal entries you may notice that you've learned quite a bit about them without having met either one. Lindsey has decided that cheerleading training, practice, and games represent tough body conditioning, but it's worth it. She says that in short sentences. She's kept photos and other mementos. When she looks back at the pages again, no matter when in her life, she will remember the hard work, but also the smiles.

Parker's life has been traumatized along with his brother Cliff's. You can see the stages of grief he lived through as he wrote short, bittersweet comments and waited for his brother to come home. He is *shocked*, he cries, he is *angry*, he cries, he feels *guilt* (why him instead of me?), more tears, he has depression and takes a day off. Slowly he forms *acceptance* of his brother with an urge to learn sign language, and he builds *hope* as holidays with family are a time to be appreciative. Parker does have a brother, physically challenged but still very much alive. This is the stage of healthy hope toward which we must strive. In the last entry we have the sense that things will be all right for them. It is the fortunate family in which there are siblings to share. Healthy adjustments to life's changes result when individuals share their pain.

How Do We Change
Our Family's Habits?

Many people feel that they cannot change their family. They may feel that their parents are too headstrong, that "they do what they want anyway" and don't pay attention to their children. Some feel that their brothers or sisters don't care, that they do what they want to do, as well. This may all be true in your family situation. The feelings are common everywhere and in all forms of family units.

However, there is one thing you can always change: You can always choose to change your mind. You can always choose to change your attitude toward your family members. Remember the war against drugs slogan: *Just say no*. The same applies to everything in your life if you say NO to the negative and say YES to only positive things.

Mack R. Douglas wrote a book back in 1966, *How to Make a Habit of Succeeding*, which has been reprinted almost thirty times. In it he says many wonderfully positive things: "Your key for personal success for today is imagination, the power and motivation of a magnificent mind . . . hunts for the ideal solution . . . and has the power to change what it has found . . ."

For a few moments after reading this page, go and sit in an entirely quiet place. Relax, and daydream the best possible pictures of what your family would be like if it were perfect. Here are a few teasing images to get you started.

Patrick

Instead of a physical challenge, I wish my brother was normal. I wish he could participate in sports, drive a car when he turns sixteen, and laugh all the time instead of cry.

Miguel

Instead of fighting, I dream of the day that my parents get along.

Marclette

Instead of always feeling that something is wrong, I feel happy and free.

Tomas

Instead of feeling sorry for my injured sister, I dream we are back to being the sibling team we used to be. We scream and fight like we used to. We wrestle and tickle each other until our sides hurt. I liked being her brother then.

Anita

Instead of dreading going home every night, I dream that I look forward to a house filled with fun. I like that idea.

Pay Attention to Your Heart

Often our hearts dream a little dream, wish a little wish, and we just stuff that wish right back inside where it came from. Because of our responsibilities in dealing with physical challenges, we forget to be happy. We forget to dream. We don't allow ourselves to sing a song or whistle a tune. Why? Why are other people happy and we are not?

We can be happy. We can make our dreams come true every single day, inch by inch, step by step, a day at a time. We cannot always change everything about our lives and the lives of our loved ones. But we can always make a switch in our own minds.

Julius

My brother has AIDS. Clint gets sick and never seems to get better. He is weak and cannot do what he used to do at the beginning of high school. He's eighteen now and can't graduate on time. He can't keep up even with the home-teacher's tutoring. He keeps falling asleep during study time. I'm in ninth grade now and try to help him. It's so hard. He tried drugs with some people just one time. But that one time they shared a needle among ten people. My brother got high and got AIDS. My mother works three jobs now, to pay for the new treatment they're trying at our clinic. My aunt has moved in with us to help take care of my brother Clint. Our lives are shattered because of drugs. I have decided I will never touch a drug unless a doctor orders it for me. I'll just say no. That's it. No talk, no other decision. I have made up my mind. That negative, ugly path is not how *my* life is going to go. I think I'm going to be a research scientist. I want to help find a cure for my brother. I just hope he lives until I can.

Julius cannot change his brother's condition, but he understands. He makes decisions for himself based on what he has learned from his family situation. That is what you can do as well. You cannot change other people's behavior, but you can express yourself. You can say what's on your mind. You can try to understand. You can treat your family members with the kindness and peace you *wish* and *dream* they would show toward you.

Get Yourself Started

The above examples of daydreams can get you started on your own path of change in attitude. For instance, because your sibling has a physical disability, does that really mean he or she can never drive a car? The answer may be yes because of the extent of physical limitations. But technology has come an incredibly long way. Begin a campaign of learning. Find out what it would cost to change your family vehicle into a driveable car for your sibling. Cost may not have to be a factor; try asking a business to donate part of the cost. Perhaps get an extra job for a while to help attain your dream for your sibling.

In doing for your sibling, you grow yourself. Dreams can and do come true!

Patrick, Again

My brother lost his leg above the knee to a sarcoma type of cancer. They couldn't save his knee, but he has a prosthesis with a bendable knee joint! I'm going to get him to sign up for the basketball league with me. I know he's good at shooting hoops, but our family has put his life on hold for way too long. It's time to get back into sports—one of our favorite loves!

Instead of wishing your parents wouldn't fight, try helping them get a night off. Many times parents are on edge because they are simply tired. Create a situation where two dreams come true: your parents get a break (you know you can handle it one night every couple of weeks), and you see them get along better.

Instead of always feeling as if something is wrong, decide to see the "right" in every single day. If a sad thought comes into your head, just say no. Tell yourself you want to see the successes that your brother or sister makes every day. You want to see the glass of water half full rather than half empty.

Tomas, Again

Instead of feeling sorry for my sister, not treating her the way I used to, I'm going to get back to the way I *really* am! I'm going to start joking, teasing her, to make her laugh. If she looks like she's going to take it the wrong way, I'm going to tell her exactly how I feel: I like her! Then I'm going to tickle her until she screams for air! Just because she has eczema and has rashes all over her body doesn't mean her ticklebones don't work!

Anita, Again

I used to dread coming home. But since I took over the dessert-making around the house, things have changed! I look forward to my next creation! I've been showing my little brother how to make stuff too. It's like this special thing we do together. We make messes, get chocolate on our faces as we lick the beaters, but we have a blast! Who says life can't be fun even when your little brother becomes deaf?

Point of View

If you go to another room, you can't see what you saw just a minute ago. When you change where you look inside your home, you change your viewpoint. The same is true when you decide to turn your mind around, decide to think differently and change to an everyday-positive attitude. Relatives will notice that you don't get angry at little things as you used to, because you don't see things the same way. The new way you act because of your new point of view causes changes in the other members of your family. Perhaps you choose not to fight with your sister even though she still yells at you. Soon she will stop yelling at you because you don't fight back; you choose to pay attention to her in a different way, such as making time to play her favorite game with her every other day. Your change affects others. That is how you can get your family to change its individual habits. Remember that how you speak to someone affects how they reply. How you act toward someone affects how they act in return.

Love, Again

Remember the biggest goal of all: everyone needs and loves love. Treating your family as you'd like to be treated—with love, with understanding—creates a much different family environment than simply fighting back because life is hard. Try loving each and every individual in your family again. No matter what has happened, choose to make your future better. Love again. Love again. Then love some more.

CHAPTER 14

Celebrate Often, It Creates Hope!

Families need time together to discuss how things are going. Typically, families do this during mealtimes. When everyone is gathered around the table, it is an excellent opportunity to review each other's lives. Since you are trying to enjoy your food, however, focus on positive, joyful items.

All too often, however, schedules prevent a complete household from sitting down to a family meal. Then the opportunity to call a family meeting should be seized any time the group is together. Perhaps driving to a church function, or to a restaurant, would be a great time to compliment someone on his accomplishments. Whenever your clan comes together is the right time to celebrate, to underline the greatness of each sibling, each parent.

In *Living, Loving and Learning*, Dr. Leo Buscaglia wrote a full chapter on: "What Is Essential Is Not Visible to the Eye." In it he talks of the "inner trip." This is how we're growing inside, as we develop our inner "self." So many of our accomplishments go unnoticed or are taken for granted. We do this not only to others, but to ourselves. It is time to take notice! It is the season to give yourself a hug for doing all your homework (especially since you had to fight the urge to drop everything and go outside . . .). You are a special, unique person. Point that out to your family. As you get older, it doesn't seem appropriate to run home screaming, "Mommy, Mommy, look at me!" but your need is as strong as ever to share your life and those of your brothers and sisters, Mom and Dad. If you find yourself moping along, not knowing what is troubling you, it may simply be that you need a compliment.

Give a Warm-fuzzy Right Now!

If you keep a positive-attitude change going, you'll find you will receive more compliments. The way to encourage positive strokes is treating others as you'd like to be treated. Beginning at home, complimenting your physically challenged sibling is a terrific "warm-fuzzy" beginning.

"Warm-fuzzies" are short, positive statements given to people to make them feel warm, cozy, and loved way inside. It is another way to have a mini-celebration. It is a spotlight to make someone feel good, to show that you are noticing how wonderful he truly is. It's a piñata without a party, yet the party spirit is there!

Rory

I feel open and honest about my sister Jessica. She's twenty now and has MS. When she began to mature at twelve, she began to have problems with her sight. Her left arm went numb every couple of days. We were all worried and confused. Then the doctors said she has multiple sclerosis. We hoped she'd go into remission— you know, be cured of it for a time. But ever since her twelfth birthday she has lost more and more feeling in her limbs, and she is confined to a wheelchair now. But her mind is strong and she can go to the bathroom on her own. That has been such a worry of hers; she so wants to be independent. She can feed herself, although her arms are unsteady and she spills a lot. I am embarrassed today because I asked a new girl over. Her parents are dropping her off at our house to study. I haven't had a chance to explain Jessica to my new friend. I hope she can handle it. Usually I am honest and explain Jessica's situation, ending with the fact that her mind is terrific and that I love her and am proud to be her brother. But I didn't have a chance to fill Alexa in on all this. I hope she makes Jessica feel okay.

Celebrate to Accent the Positive!

Abolishing embarrassment and fear is a problem people with disabled relatives must face. Feelings are hurt when people don't act with tact or sensitivity. Most of the time, others simply do not understand. Rory has the right attitude when he says that he is usually honest, explaining his family situation. That is an excellent way to incorporate your friends into the handicapped world. Along with it can go a simple statement when your friends are face to face with your sibling that accents his or her accomplishments. This is celebrating life, not being a braggart.

Rory, Again

I am relieved the evening went so well. I really liked the way Alexa handled meeting my sister. I was introducing Jessica, saying that she's a junior majoring in science, in the hope of conducting research to find a way to stop the progression of MS, when Alexa chimed in, saying that her first love is science. So they talked for a couple of minutes about chemistry; we have labs in our freshman classes similar to college labs. Wow, Alexa was so accepting. She picked up on Jessica's talents and loves, not her disability. I think I'm going to like this new girl!

To Celebrate

By definition, to celebrate means:

> To honor; to demonstrate satisfaction; to hold up for public acclaim.

Most of us consider a celebration a party, which it can be. However, mini-celebrations happen every day. Reasons for a celebration, or a pat-on-the-back, are countless. Simply being sensitive to positive events will give you reasons for joy day after day. Rory celebrated Jessica's talents in his introduction. He did not simply say: "This is my sister, she is in a wheelchair because she has multiple sclerosis." No, he affirmed her personhood, her "self," behind the outward appearance. He introduced the sister he knows and loves. That is commemorating a physically challenged person's life. That is focusing on Jessica's able-bodied traits. Physically challenged people are more than their obvious disabilities. Rory took the lead and turned a potentially uneasy introduction into a moment of genuine sharing between two people and their common interests. Multiple sclerosis aside, the two young women have commonalities. Most of us have something in common with one another. Finding those commonalities can be an interesting, challenging hobby.

Make Celebrations a Habit

Everyone likes a party. So too, you may define celebrate as:

To take part in a festival; to honor by refraining from ordinary business; to observe a notable occasion with festivities.

Go ahead. Bake a cake. Make a favorite dinner dish. Hold a party for an accomplishment. Rory could have a small celebration every time his sister completes another course toward her degree. He knows Jessica's efforts are twice those of the average student in her classes. She needs support. Better yet, she needs a boost. A semester celebration can make her feel special. It makes Rory feel special too, because he is making his sister feel good, helping her grow in spite of her challenges.

Hope

When a family concentrates on the successes of its members, hope shines in on the total family. Through all the stages of grief, with all the reasons we have to go through the grief process over and over again, the goal is finally to grow to a state of hope. The future is brighter because of our pain. Wonderful things do remain for us to enjoy.

Hope allows us to see the beauty of the complete forest and all of its precious trees.

J.P.

My little brother was caught in the fire that burned down our apartment building five years ago. He was burned over half of his face and both of his hands and arms. He was ten at the time. He has had five years of skin grafts and healing and surgery to reconstruct his face. His nose was almost completely burned off. He can't smell anything. Considering how badly he was hurt, how many infections he's had to fight, he's doing beautifully. He looks different. He has scars on his face and hands. Parts of his fingers burned off, so he has ten shorter fingers, healed down to the first joints. But he is very much alive. You know how a little kid can drive you nuts? Well, Julius can do that with me and he's fifteen, which isn't so little! I'm seventeen and, you know, I wouldn't trade my brother for anything, or anyone. Sure, I had those sick feelings inside when I went to see him in the hospital day after day, month after month, thinking the infection would kill him. But God has given him a very special something, a faith in himself to get through this that has never wavered. Many days Julius has cheered *me* up, telling *me* not to cry, not to worry. I still can't believe how strong he is. His strength has paid off for our whole family. My older brothers who are married and have little ones all join us in pulling Julius up when he is down. And he does get down. But his past strength gives us more determination to see him through anything—from the stupidest remarks about his scars to the fact that playing the piano is extremely difficult for him. As far as I can see, Julius isn't handicapped at all. It is all the other people who don't notice his talent, who don't notice his inner faith, who don't acknowledge that he has human feelings, who are the handicapped ones. They have boxed-in their minds, they don't think freely. My brother Julius and I are free. We know we can live through anything now. We know how fine the air can feel on our faces, how soft the fur of a kitten is to our touch. These things Julius could not always appreciate because of his pain. I am so grateful that he has healed and has no more pain. You can see in his eyes the enjoyment he gets from so many things. I am definitely a better person because I have my little brother in my life.

Pain Causes Grief Causes Pain

The unfortunate cycle of pain following a trauma frequently triggers a long, continuing circle of grief. J.P. describes the freedom his brother and family feel because Julius is healed. If you have a relative who is in constant pain, looking for hope may seem a never-ending search Outside help can bring you and your family hope.

Suggestions for Becoming Free from Pain

1. Make sure all that is possible is being done by your doctors (surgery and treatments).
2. Understand that pain medication may be needed on a long-term basis; drugs are not all bad.
3. Watch for side effects from medications; discuss your observations with your family and doctors.
4. Keep busy; keep your sibling involved physically and mentally as much as possible.
5. Consult a counselor on how to cope day by day

with pain; there are methods that work. Training the mind is an important life skill.

6. Read about pain; there are many studies and books on pain management.

7. Although you may not want to, allow your physically challenged sibling to be alone sometimes, to try to cope on his own.

8. Try not to take angry outbursts as attacks on you; it's the pain talking.

9. Seek relief and support in a group, medical/support personnel, church members, other patients' families.

10. If an organized group is not available, ask medical people for names of others in your situation; meet, share, begin helping others, and they will help you to take time out to become renewed.

There Is Always Hope

We will not understand everything in this life. Using our energy to try to figure out why can be extremely draining and hazardous to our own health and well-being. Rather, if we try to accept what we cannot change and use our energies to learn from every sad and tragic experience we face, we will make wise use of the energy we do have. In seeking help through learning, we pave our own road of hope. Showing we still have hope can make all the difference to our physically challenged sibling, our family and friends.

CHAPTER 15

What If Your Brother or Sister Dies?

The saddest of all things when tragedy strikes a family is the fear of death. And that is what we fear most when an accident, illness, or a birth defect occurs: Will the person die? What will I do? Although this is not something that most people want to talk about, discussing it is of the utmost importance if we are to understand the physically challenged person in our lives. Reading and talking about death is a primary need for those of us who live with a physically challenged sibling.

Fear

Commonly, fear of death blocks us from dealing with death. Although we know that we will all die one day, it is our firm belief that we will make it to a hundred years or more. We see more and more people retiring and living for thirty, forty, and fifty years longer.

This longevity, however, encourages us to put off thinking about and understanding death in a personal way. Then, something and someone changes our lives. Reluctantly, we must think about the death of a loved one. The possibility of one's own death and that of other loved ones also comes to mind.

Larisa

My brother Ivy died last month. He was fifteen and a hemophiliac. That means he was born with a lack of the clotting factor in his blood. Even the smallest cut can cause excessive bleeding in hemophiliacs. That didn't stop Ivy! He used to just go about life, playing sports and trying to live normally. If he got hurt, he'd have to try to stop the bleeding. Several times he had to go to the hospital and receive transfusions to replace the blood he had lost. That's how he contracted the virus that causes AIDS. This was before they knew how to screen donated blood for AIDS. We didn't find out about the virus being in his system until he got cut in football and the cut became infected. It didn't heal, so he went into the hospital for the tenth time, and his blood tested HIV-positive. Although he fought the infection and other sicknesses with great determination, the last problem was overwhelming. He died of pneumonia because his body could not fight any longer. I have been angry that all his life he fought to stay well, and in fighting hemophilia he contracts a deadly disease. I miss him. I dream about him all the time. In one dream I remember being afraid that I would get AIDS. When I woke up I knew better. You

can't get AIDS by living in the same house with someone.
But I've been thinking. As I begin my senior year, I think
I'm going to study medicine. If necessary, I'll study and
work at the same time. I have to try to help find a cure for
AIDS. I don't know why Ivy was taken away, but I do
know I want to dedicate part of my life to him. In my
heart I've talked to Ivy. He's pleased, I know it.

No One Can Take It All Away

Larisa is right. You can sense things. You can talk to loved
ones in your mind, in your heart. Life is more than
physical; we are all given a mental/spiritual level of life.
As humans we have abilities more complex and more
wonder-filled than those of the animals. Let us use our
gift of memory to keep a loved one who dies always with
us in our thoughts. If you realize this before the death of
a close one, then make sure you enjoy each other in the
present. Invent reasons to take photos. Make up causes to
sit and sip a favorite drink together. Share yourself and
your time with your physically challenged sibling. Know
that in the sharing, joy is found. Precious moments can
never be taken away from you. Make as many as you can.

When Will I Die?

Any one of us can become physically challenged. An accident can happen at any time. We don't know when we
will die, but you surely know that you are alive right now.
Try some of the ideas mentioned in this book, change
your thoughts of anger or negativity to ones of joy—just
because you are alive. Fear of dying can prevent us from
living. Fear of your brother's dying can make you turn
away. If your sister were to die tomorrow, would you be

able to say that you've spent special, personal moments together, that you knew her well?

THE TAKE-CHARGE CHART	
Reaction/Feeling	Positive Action
I don't want to see my sibling like this	Go see your sibling; if you cry, then share the fact that you're sad along with her.
I don't want to talk at all	Just sit with your brother; even holding a hand can be a comfort to you both.
I hate it all	Take a big break; ask your family for time-off; be honest with your physically challenged sibling. Often, he or she will be happy you are not giving up your life to him.
I'm sick of my routine	Change your routine. Talk to your family; they probably could use a change as well. Refreshed, you will help your sibling better.
I'm afraid. I don't want you to die.	Tell your sibling this; face the fear of death together. Expressing love makes people feel loved.
I feel so helpless.	Tell your loved one this; share a game or an activity; ask if there is something she'd rather do.
Don't scream at me!	Tell this to your sibling; tell him it hurts to be yelled at; tell him you want to understand but can't if you keep getting hurt.
I cry and cry all night long.	It is good to let your feelings out; but if you're stuck, communicate with a parent, family member, counselor, teacher, church member, trusted adult. Get help to work it out.

Brandon

My big brother had Hodgkin's disease. He was twenty-three. Chip wrote poems. I used to love asking him if he had written a new one today, because toward the end of his life he did a lot of writing. Because of his disease, which involves swelling of many organs and lymph nodes, he felt awful all this past year. He couldn't sleep, didn't want to eat much, and began having strange pains. But Chip had a gift for making me laugh. He would take me to his college hangouts to sit with his friends and tell stories and laugh until dawn. Chip couldn't drink; it made him feel sick. So we'd just watch how crazy everyone else acted when they were loaded. Chip and I went to zillions of places together. I have ten booklets of his poems. I understood him because I understood what he wrote. When he had something important to say, he'd write it. Then he'd get me to read it, and I would tell him I knew how he felt. He knew I knew. He crashed on his motorcycle and died instantly. I think it was not an accident. I think he just couldn't live with his body any more. He didn't leave me a suicide note, but his last poems were filled with despair. He saw no way out of a future of pain and illness. He didn't want us to live though that either. So he died. I miss him every single hour. I'm going to publish his books. So much of his work was filled with life!

Is Suicide Wrong?

Chip's influence is carrying on in Brandon's life. But suicide exists. It is a way out that some have chosen. There are countless other choices besides suicide. If you have felt depressed enough to end it all, seek help. Given the precious chance for life, try not to waste your opportunity. Many people have felt deep depression and can help you live through it.

But if you have a close one who you think has taken his or her life, seek help for yourself. So many questions are left unanswered when someone leaves us voluntarily. Do we understand how desperate a person is, especially one who is not well? Probably not.

The most that we can do for our family is to love them and be there for them. We cannot live other people's lives for them. As tempting as it may be to devote your life to your sibling, you are not in charge of that person's life, only your own. Holding hands during stress and tragedy, sharing the life we have together is the very best we can do. If you are uncomfortable in your situation, talk to someone outside your family for help in continuing to do the best you can.

Communicating about Death

Again, communicating your feelings about your fears helps you face them. We humans seem to want to avoid pain and unhappiness. But in telling pain, a surprising *comfort* can come over you. Sharing your feelings however you can is the start to facing your fears. In discussing your personal questions about death, you are taking part in a needed change. We all must learn that life is fragile and must be lived while we can live it! Sad or happy, it is your life to live.

A Special Kind of Love

Maria

When I was little, I found a tiny kitten crawling around under our porch. I fed her milk with an eye-dropper. I washed her fur gently with mild soap every day, to get all the bugs and germs off. Slowly, she began to grow. I called her Little Tigra, because her coloring was orange-yellow with black markings like a big tiger. I would brush her coat and put different colored ribbons around her neck. She was fully trained and stayed in our garage. One day she just ran away. She might be dead. She might just be lost. I miss her, and because I took care of her, I feel so close to kittens now. I'd like to have another kitten to love someday.

Caring Is Caring

Just like caring for a pet, parents care for their babies. Just like parents in many ways, we care for our brothers and sisters. We watch out for each other. We argue and disagree, but we learn to get along as we grow up. This kind of connection with a living soul is the special bonding that comes from providing care. When you take care of someone, you love him or her in a very personal and intimate way. For those of you who have pets, that closeness is very similar. Caring for family is a bond that lasts throughout your life.

Zoryanna

When Nicki became ill, our family's life changed. He was found to have leukemia, but he appears to be in remission at present after an operation to remove his spleen. He is back in school, attending sixth grade at the age of twelve. At times, I miss seeing him and reading to him. That may sound strange. I do not miss the *sick* Nicki, just the closeness we felt during the long weeks of his acute illness. I am going to begin again to make time to be with him, to read and laugh and enjoy each other. I hate to think that people have to get sick in our family to take time for each other.

To Give Is to Receive More in Return

Dr. Jampolsky in his book *Teach Only Love* writes in a chapter about giving: "When our attention is on the giving and joining with others, fear is removed and we accept healing for ourselves." Many of us have been taught this important lesson within the framework of the Bible. No matter what your religion, this rule is almost universal: "It is better to give than to receive." Zoryanna has lived this maxim, realizing that she received a special kind of love while caring for her brother. She has made the distinction between her newfound desire to be with her brother even though he is not so ill, and wanting him back in bed so she can take care of him. Certainly she doesn't wish more illness for him. In living through her brother's challenges, Zoryanna has unraveled a puzzle of life. Giving someone your time and energy is giving yourself a gift: the special love created in a caregiving relationship.

"Falling in Love" with the Doctor

Margrit

I have just loved going to Dr. Gold's with my brother Jan. Ever since he was born, Jan has had allergies. You probably think that allergies are fairly common and nothing to worry about, but Jan's are very serious. He has trouble breathing and digesting certain foods. He can't wear clothing made of anything but cotton, nor can it be washed in any soap with fragrance in it. He has spent the last thirteen years of his life trying to find out what he's allergic to, so my parents can get rid of it as much as possible in our home environment. I've always gone to Dr. Gold's with Jan because my parents have wanted us to understand why we have to watch our lives so closely— for the sake of Jan's health. But I loved going to see his doctor anyway. He is always there at the other end of the telephone with advice and care when Jan has one of his violent reactions. Jan has asthma too, and has attacks so bad that he cannot breathe. We have to rush him to the hospital, where he stays until whatever is causing his reaction is cleared from his air passageways. Doctor Gold is always there. He really gives us a lot of thought and care. He will always be my favorite doctor.

Margrit tells of another example of the special feelings you experience when you've gone through a traumatic situation with someone. Their family doctor has cared for Jan for years. He has become a special part of Margrit's life because he gives help, support, and care to their entire family when they are in need. It is quite common to feel a special fondness for our good doctors. They help us make it through some of life's most difficult times.

You Have More Energy Than You Think

Are you thinking you have *had it* with giving? Perhaps your point of view would change if you considered what life would be like without your family members. What would you do if you didn't have those personal moments with your brother, your one-on-one time with your sister?

Day-to-day struggles make our lives a continual comparison of what I want and what I don't want. It's draining to have to deal with crisis after crisis at home. But if, as Larisa has experienced, it were all taken away, would that make you happier? Most of us would easily answer no, we would not want our physically challenged brother or sister to die or be taken away. As much as our energy is expended, it is worth the special love we develop by helping a person live well.

Difficult Life

M. Scott Peck begins his book *The Road Less Traveled* (a book about inner growth): "Life is difficult. . . . This is a great truth. . . . Once we truly know that life is difficult . . . then life is no longer [so] difficult . . . once . . . accepted, the fact that life is difficult no longer matters."

For those of you with a physical challenge in your lives, those words are so very clear. For those who have experienced a personal trauma, a tragedy close to home, those words ring with truth.

Okay. You have a physical challenge in your life. Acceptance of it is half the battle. The other half of life is how to make the challenge an opportunity.

How do we use what we have had to learn?

How do we take our understanding and make it work for us?

Choosing the path is up to you. Keeping your focus positive is your choice as well. Being constructive, perhaps by becoming an advocate for the physically challenged, could be a path you choose for part of your time. Whatever your choices, base them on the love you've experienced through your family challenges.

Life is difficult. You've handled it. Within that handling with care, you've found a very special kind of love. The love within your family will outlast any tragedy. Brother love and sister love last lifetimes as you share with others how you've learned to care.

Glossary

able-bodied Having the ability to do many things, to function on many levels.

acceptance The fifth stage of grief; coming to terms with loss.

accomplishment Completion; attainment of a goal.

acute Severe, rapid onset; opposite of chronic.

adolescence Period from the beginning of puberty to adulthood.

advocate One who supports or pleads in favor of; to defend someone or some idea.

AIDS (acquired immune deficiency syndrome) Disorder caused by the human immunodeficiency virus (HIV); the virus permits infections, malignancies, and neurologic diseases. Most cases have been caused sharing hypodermic needles or sexual contact.

amputation Removal, by surgery or trauma, of a limb, part, or organ.

amputee One who has had a limb removed.

anger Extreme displeasure, desire to lash out, hit; second stage of grief.

asthma Difficult breathing because of a spasm of the bronchial tubes and/or mucus in them.

attitudinal healing The recovery of health (mental, physical, spiritual) due to a positive, constructive, intentional attitude adjustment toward wellness.

bargaining Making a deal (perhaps with God) in hope of restoring things to the way they were.

benign Not progressive; not cancerous.

bilateral Affecting both sides

blindness Inability to see, affecting one or both eyes; legal blindness is considered to be 20/200 or less in the best-seeing eye.

body image Picture people have of their physical appearance based on their own view and reactions of others; self-image.

brace Tool or device used to support and hold joints or limbs in place.

cancer A malignant growth; abnormal growth of abnormal cells.

cerebral palsy Paralysis resulting from developmental defects in brain or trauma at birth; movements are often spastic because of lack of control of certain muscles.

challenge To stimulate or excite into action.

chemotherapy Use of chemical medicines to kill disease-causing microorganisms; usually used in cancer treatment.

chronic Lasting a long time; opposite of acute.

clinic Center for physical examinations and treatment of outpatients.

colostomy Opening of part of the large intestine to outside of body, where a bag is attached to receive waste.

congenital Existing at birth.

counselor Person trained to provide advice and guidance for a person's mental (and thus physical) well-being.

crisis Unstable period in a person's life resulting from a traumatic event.

cystic fibrosis Inherited disease affecting the pancreas and respiratory system; characterized by continual respiratory infection, and pancreatic difficulties.

day-home Place for challenged adults to live together, independent from their relatives.

deafness Hearing loss or impairment.

defect Flaw; imperfection.

denial First stage of grief; refusal to admit reality.

depression Fourth stage of grief; altered mental mood; loss of interest in pleasurable outlets.

development Orderly growth to full size or maturity.

diabetes   Disease causing abnormal sugar levels in urine and blood; continued high levels of sugar cause difficulties in many bodily functions including sight and healing of wounds. Juvenile diabetes—onset before the age of 25—is inherited and usually difficult to regulate with diet and medication.

dialysis   Process to cleanse the blood of the kidneys.

disability   Lack of ability to do things considered in the normal range.

discriminate   To make a difference in treatment on a basis other than individual accomplishment.

Down syndrome   Moderate to severe retardation caused by genetic chromosome abnormality.

eczema   Skin condition (acute or chronic) of rashes, scales, or scabs; may be allergic reaction; can be hereditary.

epilepsy   Continuing disorder of cerebral function; symptoms are sudden, brief attacks called seizures.

extremity   End part; hand or foot.

fatigue   Extreme weariness from physical or emotional stress.

frustration   Feeling of dissatisfaction caused by wants or needs being unmet.

genuine   True; sincerely felt.

graft   Tissue taken from one portion of the body to cover wounds in another area; often used in burn victims.

grief   Emotional reaction to loss of a loved one, object, part of body, or health. Physical reactions can include overwhelming fatigue, hollow or empty feeling in chest or abdomen, sighing, shortness of breath, lump in the throat.

guilt   Part of the grief process; emotion resulting from doing what is thought to be wrong; need for punishment.

handicap   Disadvantage that makes achievement unusually difficult; mental or physical disability.

hate   Emotion often attached to anger; intense dislike of behavior or circumstance.

hearing impairment   Loss of some or all of the ability to hear; partial deafness.

hemophilia   Inherited blood disease in which the blood clotting time is greatly prolonged.

HIV Human immunodeficiency virus.

Hodgkin's disease Unknown cause of enlarged lymph tissue, spleen, and liver; affecting other tissues as well.

hope According to Elisabeth Kübler-Ross, MD, the final stage of grief.

impairment Loss of any physical or mental structure or function.

independent living Having skills to perform daily tasks; term used by medical professionals and patients that emphasizes the rehabilitation goals of active community living.

infection Invasion of the body or body part by a micro-organism.

isolation State of being alone, set apart from others.

life-curve The continuation of learning and growth throughout one's lifetime.

jealousy Hostility and at times rage at a person believed to have an advantage.

kidney Two organs that eliminate urine and help regulate the water and blood of the body by a filtering process.

kidney transplant Surgical placing of a live kidney from a donor.

leukemia Blood disorder, acute or chronic, of unknown origin; symptoms are unrestrained growth of white blood cells.

life-curve The continuation of learning and growth throughout one's lifetime.

life skills Various learned patterns of behavior that are constructive in obtaining a positive life-style of health and overall wellness.

mainstreaming Educational practice of allowing handicapped children to participate in mixed classroom settings.

malignant Cancerous.

multiple sclerosis Inflammatory disease of the nervous system with degradation of the nerves.

muscular dystrophy Wasting disease of muscles.

myoelectronic prosthesis Advanced upper limb prosthetic device operated by batteries turned on by electrodes that are attached to muscles. The movement of muscles activates the prosthesis.

orthopedics Branch of medicine dealing with prevention and correction of disorders of motion-oriented parts of body: bones, joints, muscles, other supporting structures.

orthotist Medical technician who makes corrective bracework for deformities or disabilities.

oxygen tank Container of pure oxygen to relieve immediate breathing difficulties.

Paralympics Competition for athletes with disabilities.

paraplegia Paralysis of legs and lower part of body.

pneumonia Inflammation of lungs by bacteria, viruses, or chemical irritations.

"preemie" Nickname for a premature baby.

prosthesis (prŏs THĒ sĭs) Artificial replacement for a missing body part; plural, prostheses.

prosthetics Branch of medicine dealing with creating and replacing missing parts of body.

prosthetist Medical specialist who studies the body and engineering to create well-fitted tools to replace missing limbs, organs, or teeth.

psychologist One trained in mental processes and behaviors, analysis, therapy, and research.

psychiatrist Medical doctor trained in diagnosis, treatment, and prevention of mental illness.

puberty Period of life at which members of both sexes become capable of reproduction.

quadriplegia Paralysis of all four extremities and usually the trunk of the body.

rehabilitation Process of education and treatment that leads a disabled patient to attain maximum function, a sense of well-being, and a personally satisfying level of independent living.

remission Period during which symptoms of a disease disappear.

residual Remaining after an illness or injury.

robotic Nickname for myoelectronic prosthesis.

sarcoma Cancer arising from connective tissue such as bone and muscle.

scoliosis Unusual curve, rather than straight growth, of the spine.

seizure Sudden attack of a disease, as in epileptic convulsion; involuntary muscle contraction and relaxation due to cerebral malfunction.

self-worth Positive feelings toward one's talents and value.

siblings Children of the same parents; brothers and sisters.

spastic Having uncontrollable, sudden movement or convulsive muscular contraction, usually resulting from disease or malfunction.

spina bifida Congenital defect of walls of spinal canal; lack of union between some vertebrae, with spinal cord protruding through opening, forming a tumor.

support group Gathering of people to share common experiences and try to help each other live through their experiences.

therapist Specialist skilled in treating and training a person with a disease or injury back to fullest functioning potential.

trauma Disordered mental or behavioral state resulting from mental or emotional stress or physical injury.

voicebox Larynx, the organ of speech.

Appendix

Resource List

AIDS Information
1132 West Peachtree Street, NW
Atlanta, GA 30309
Hotlines: 1-800-342-2437; 1-800-551-2728

American Amputee Foundation
P.O. Box 55218, Hillcrest Station
Little Rock, AR 72225

American Cancer Society National Office
1599 Clifton Road, NE
Atlanta, GA 30329

American Diabetes Association
1660 Duke Street
Alexandria, VA 22314
1-800-232-3472

American Foundation for the Blind
15 West 16th Street
New York, NY 10011

Amputee Foundation of Greater Atlanta
120 Shady Brooke Walk
Fairburn, GA 30213

American Amputee Foundation (AAF)
701 West 7th Street
Little Rock, AR 72201

ARISE (Alternatives for Reaching Independence through Services and Engineering)
501 East Fayette Street
Syracuse, NY 13202

Cystic Fibrosis Foundation
6931 Arlington Road
Bethesda, MD 20814
1-800-344-4823

Epilepsy Foundation of America
4351 Garden City Drive
Landover, MD 20785-2267
1-800-EFA-1000

Fifty-Two Association for the Handicapped, Inc. (a sports association)
441 Lexington Avenue
New York, NY 10017

Leukemia Society of America National Headquarters
733 Third Avenue
New York, NY 10017

Muscular Dystrophy Association
3561 East Sunrise Drive
Tucson, AZ 85718

National Amputee Golf Association
P.O. Box 1228
Amherst, NH 03031

National Down Syndrome Congress
1800 Dempster Street
Park Ridge, IL 60068-1146

National Down Syndrome Society
666 Broadway
New York, NY 10012
1-800-221-4602

National Handicapped Sports and Recreation Association
(NHSRA)
P.O. Box 33141, Farragut Station
Washington, DC 20033

National Hemophilia Foundation
110 Greene Street
New York, NY 10012

National Information Center for Handicapped Children and
Youths (NICHCY)
P.O. Box 1492
Washington, DC 20013

National Kidney Foundation
30 East 33rd Street
New York, NY 10016

National Organization on Disability
2100 Pennsylvania Avenue NW
Washington, DC 20037

National Rehabilitation Association
1910 Association Drive
Alexandria, VA 22091

National Scoliosis Foundation (NSF)
93 Concord Avenue
Belmont, MA 02178

New York Orthotic and Prosthetics Association (NYOPA)
50 Main Street
White Plains, NY 10606

PACT (Parents of Amputee Children)
Kessler Institute for Rehabilitation
Pleasant Valley Way
West Orange, NJ 07052

Paralympics
555 Ralph McGill Boulevard
Atlanta, GA 30312

Roosevelt Warm Springs Institute for Rehabilitation
P.O. Box 1000
Warm Springs, GA 31830-0268

Spina Bifida Association of America
1700 Rockville Pike
Rockville, MD 20852
1-800-621-3141

United Cerebral Palsy Association
7 Penn Plaza
New York, NY 10001
1-800-872-1827

For Further Reading

Books

Adams, B. *Like It Is: Facts and Feelings about Handicaps from Kids to You.* New York: Walker & Co., 1979.

Allen, George N. *Ri.* New York: Prentice-Hall, 1978. (Korean boy with amputation adopted by American soldier)

Anderson, Peggy. *Children's Hospital.* Harper & Row, 1985.

Area Child Amputee Center. *Children with Limb Loss.* (Handbook series for children and adults) Grand Rapids, MI: 235 Wealthy Street SE.

Blank, J. *Nineteen Steps Up the Mountain: The Story of the DeBolt Family.* Philadelphia: J.B. Lippincott, 1976.

Brazelton, B.T. *Infants and Mothers.* New York: Dell Publishing, 1969.

————. *Toddlers and Parents.* New York: Dell Publishing, 1974.

Brown, T., and Ortiz, F. *Someone Special Just Like You.* New York: Holt, Rinehart & Winston, 1984.

Butler, D. *Cushla and Her Books.* Boston: Horn Book, 1980.

Buscaglia, Leo. *The Disabled and Their Parents: A Counseling Challenge.* New York: Holt, Rinehart & Winston, 1983.

————. *Living, Loving, and Learning.* New York: Ballantine Books/Random House, 1983.

————. *Because I Am Human.* Thorofare, NJ: Charles B. Slack, 1972.

Cleland, J. Max. *Strong at the Broken Places.* Marietta, GA: Cherokee Publishers, 1980.

Gosgrove, James. *Cap'n Smudge "So if you see someone dif-*

ferent than you and me." Los Angeles: Price/Stern/Sloan, 1982.

Deford, Frank. *Alex: The Life of a Child.* Cystic Fibrosis Foundation, P.O. Box 96476, Washington, DC 20077-7215.

Desmarowitz, Dorothea. *Martin Is Our Friend.* Nashville, TN: Abingdon Press.

Dickman, Irving. *One Miracle at a Time: How to Get Help for Your Disabled Child.* New York: Simon & Schuster, 1985.

Donavan, Peter. *Carol Johnston: The One-Armed Gymnast.* Chicago: Children's Press, 1982.

Douglas, Mack. *How to Make a Habit of Succeeding.* Grand Rapids, MI: Zondervan Publishing, 1966.

Dreikurs, R., and Satz, V. *Children: The Challenge.* New York: Hawthorne Books, 1964.

Fanshaw, E. *Rachel.* Scarsdale, NY: Bradbury Press, 1975.

Featherstone, H. *A Difference in the Family Life with a Disabled Child.* New York: Basic Books, 1980.

Feingold, S.N., and Miller, N. *Your Future: A Guide for the Handicapped Teenager.* New York: Richards Rosen Press, 1982.

Ferris, Caren. *A Hug Isn't Enough.* Washington, DC: Gallaudet College Press.

Finston, Peggy. *Parenting Plus: Raising Children with Special Health Needs.* New York: Penguin Books, 1990.

Forecki, Marcia Calhoun. *Speak to Me.* Washington, DC: Gallaudet College Press.

Gaes, Jason. *My Book for Kids with Cansur, A Child's Autobiography of Hope.* Aberdeen, SD: Melius & Peterson Publishing Corp., 1987.

Gallagher, Hugh G. *FDR's Splendid Deception.* New York: Dodd, Mead Publishers, 1984–85.

Gliedman, J., and Roth, W. *The Unexpected Minority: Handicapped Children in America.* New York: Harcourt Brace Jovanovich, 1980.

Goodshell, J. *Daniel Inouye.* New York: Cromwell Publishing, 1977.

Grollman, Sharon. *Shira: A Legacy of Courage.* New York: Doubleday & Co.

Howe, J. *The Hospital Book.* New York: Crown Publishers, 1981.

Ilg, F., Ames, L., and Baker, S. *Child Behavior.* New York: Barnes & Noble, 1981.

Jampolski, Gerald, MD. *Teach Only Love.* New York: Bantam Books, 1993.

Kamien, J. *What If I Couldn't . . . ? A Book about Special Needs.* New York: Charles Scribner's Sons, 1979.

Kaufman, C. *Rajesh.* New York: Atheneum Books, 1985.

Kegal, B. *Sports for the Leg Amputee.* Redmond, WA: Medic Publishing Co., 1986.

Kersey, K. *Helping Your Child Handle Stress.* Washington, DC: Acropolis Books, Ltd., 1986.

Kubler-Ross, Elisabeth, MD. *On Death and Dying.* New York: Macmillan, 1969.

Litchfield, Ada. *Captain Hook, That's Me.* New York: Walker & Co., 1982.

Mack, N. *Tracy.* Milwaukee: Raintree Publisher, 1976.

MacLachlen, P. *Through Grandpa's Eyes.* New York: Harper & Row, 1980.

McConnell, N. *Different and Alike.* Colorado Springs: Current, Inc., 1982.

McCormick, D. *The Incredible Mr. Kavanaugh.* New York: Devin-Adair, 1961.

Meyer, D., and Fewell, R. *Living with a Brother or Sister with Special Needs.* Seattle: University of Washington Press, 1985.

Meyers, Jeff. *One of a Kind.* Maryland Heights, MO: Sunrise Publishing, 1980.

Miezio, P. *Parenting Children with Diabilities: A Professional Source for Physicians and a Guide for Parents.* Levittown, PA: Phoenix Society, 1983.

Miller, M.S. *Child-Stress! Understanding and Answering Stress Signals of Infants, Children, and Teenagers.* New

York: Doubleday, 1982.

Newth, Philip. *Roly Goes Exploring*. New York: Philomel Books, 1981.

Nicholson, W. *Pete Gray: One-Armed Major Leaguer*. Englewood Cliffs, NJ: Prentice-Hall.

Nordic Committee on Disability. *The More We Do Together*. New York: World Rehabilitation Fund, 1985.

Peck, M. Scott, MD. *The Road Less Traveled*. New York: Simon & Schuster/Touchstone, 1978.

Raab, Robert. *Coping with Death*. New York: Rosen Publishing Group, 1989.

Rabe, Berneice. *The Balancing Girl*. New York: E.P. Dutton, 1981.

Richter, E. *The Teenage Hospital Experience*. New York: Cowan, McCann Geoghegan, 1982.

Rogers, F. *Josephine the Short-Neck Giraffe*. Pittsburgh: Family Communications, Inc.

Routburg, Marcia. *On Becoming a Special Parent, A Mini-Support Group in a Book*. Chicago: Parent/Professional Publications.

Sargent, S., and West, D.A. *My Favorite Place*. Nashville, TN: Abingdon Press, 1983.

Setouguchi, Y., and Rosenfelder, R. *The Limb Deficient Child*. Springfield, IL: Charles C. Thomas, Publisher.

Siegel, Bernie, MD. *Love, Medicine and Miracles*. New York: Harper & Row, 1986.

———. *Peace, Loving and Healing*. New York: Harper & Row, 1989.

Silber, John R. *Shooting Straight: What's Wrong with America and How to Fix It*. New York: Harper & Row, 1989.

Simons, Robin. *After the Tears. Parents Talk about Raising a Child with a Disability*. Orlando, FL: Harcourt Brace Jovanovich, 1987.

Stein, B. *About Handicaps: An Open Family Book for Parents and Children*. New York: Walker & Co., 1984.

Sullivan, Brightman, Blatt, Roberts, Williams, Fiske. *Feeling*

Free. Reading, MA: Addison-Wesley, 1979.

Sutcliff, Rosemary. *Warrior Scarlet*. New York: Henry L. Walch Publishers, 1958.

Swigget, Howard. *The Extraordinary Mr. Morris*. Garden City, NY: Country Life Press, 1952.

Tate, J. *Ben and Annie*. New York: Doubleday, 1974.

Trull, P. *On with My Life*. New York: Putnam, 1983.

Voight, C. *Izzy-Willy-Nilly*. New York: Atheneum Books, 1986.

Waller, S. *Circle of Hope*. New York: Evans Publishing Company, 1981.

Weisinger, H. *Anger Work-Out Book*. New York: William Morrow & Co., 1985.

Westburg, G. *Good Grief*. Philadelphia: Fortress Press, 1962.

Whipple, Lee. *Whole Again*. Ottawa, IL: Green Hill Publishers.

Wieland, Bob, with Sarah Nichols Brown. *One Step at a Time*. Grand Rapids, MI: Zondervan Publishers, 1989.

Wolf, B. *Don't Feel Sorry for Paul*. New York: J.B. Lippincott, 1974.

Yolen, Jane. *The Seeing Stick*. New York: Thomas Y. Crowell, 1977.

Periodicals and Newsletters

Amputee Foundation of
    Greater Atlanta; Newsletter
120 Shady Brooke Walk
Fairburn, GA 30213

IAP (Institute for the Advancement of Prosthetics)
4424 South Pennsylvania Avenue
Lansing, MI 48910-5695

Imprints, Birth and Life Bookstore Newsletter
7001 Alonzo Avenue NW
Seattle, WA 98107-0625

In Stride (Alfred I. DuPont Institute Newsletter)
1660 Rockland Road
Wilmington, DE 19899

JACPOC (Journal of the Association of Children's Prosthetic/
Orthotic Clinics)
222 South Prospect Avenue
Park Ridge, IL 60068

JPO (Journal of Prosthetics and Orthotics)
1650 King Street
Alexandria, VA 22314

O & P Experience (Insights into Orthotics and Prosthetics)
6010 McGinnis Ferry Road
Alpharetta, GA 30202

Orthotics and Prosthetics, Journal of
American Orthotic and Prosthetic Association
1650 King Street
Alexandria, VA 22314

Palestra Magazine
P.O. Box 508
McComb, IL 61455

Programs for the Handicapped (Clearinghouse on the
Handicapped)
Department of Education/Office of Special Education and
Rehabilitative Services
Washington, DC 20202

Superkids Newsletter
60 Clyde Street
Newton, MA 02160

Vermont Handicapped Ski Foundation Newsletter
P.O. Box 261
Brownsville, VT 05037

Index